DEADLY ENCOUNTERS

THE CHARGE AGAINST THE BARON DE VIDIL.

For some days past the clubs have echoed with nothing else than rumours, more or less exaggerated and incorrect, respecting the extraordinary crime with which the Baron de Vidil is now charged at Paris with having attempted to perpetrate last week. The most contradictory accounts have, in fact, been in circulation regarding this strange attempt, and they yesterday went the length of asserting that young Mr. de Vidil had died of his wounds at Twickenham. We are glad at once to be able to say that there is no ground for this latter statement. Young Mr. de Vidil, though very seriously and almost dangerously cut about the head, is making rapid progress, and is likely soon to be convalescent. We may state at the outset that for the last four days we have been in possession of all the facts that have yet transpired in connexion with the extraordinary attempt at crime. It was, however, positively necessary for the ends of justice that as little publicity as possible should be given to the details, which, though widely discussed, were generally discredited from the mere fact of nothing appearing in the public journals concerning it. Now, however, that the arrest of the Baron de Vidil is known at Paris, we have, of course, no further motive for concealment.

The Baron de Vidil is a French gentleman by birth, who, having married an English lady of fortune, has long been in the habit of visiting London, where his position and friends gave him the *entrée* to the most distinguished society in the metropolis. He was an honorary member of several of the principal clubs, and, in fact, a gentleman whose position in what is termed "society" was admitted everywhere. Baron Vidil is now accused of having attempted to murder his son last Friday week, June 28th, under circumstances of peculiar atrocity. The endless *on dits* which are current as to the cause which impelled him to this crime are often inconsistent with themselves, and nearly all irreconcilable with each other. We can only rely, therefore, on what has generally been communicated to us on what we may call emphatically "good authority." It is stated, then, that lately the Baron de Vidil has become embarrassed, and, in fact, was pressed urgently for ready money. His son is a young gentleman, 23 years of age, who has been reared almost entirely in England, and who has graduated at Cambridge. By the death of this young man the Baron de Vidil would become entitled at once to 30,000l. Whether the conduct of the Baron has ever been such as to raise suspicion in his son's mind that he ever meditated or even desired the death of his young heir it is impossible to say. This can only be known to the son himself, and, of course, can never be elicited till criminal proceedings are instituted. The facts connected with the actual attempt may be very soon told. The Baron proposed to his son that they should ride out and pay their respects to the Due d'Aumale and the members of the ex-Royal family at Claremont. Both gentlemen, accordingly, started by the train from Waterloo for Twickenham, where they hired horses and rode on to Claremont. Young Mr. Alfred De Vidil had a light riding whip, but the Baron had none. At Claremont

FRIGHTFUL ENCOUNTER IN NORTHUMBERLAND-STREET.

Between 11 and 12 o'clock yesterday a fearful scene took place at Northumberland-chambers, 16, Northumberland-street, Strand, in the apartments of Mr. J. Roberts, a solicitor and bill discounter, who occupies the first floor of that house. A deadly struggle had taken place between Mr. Roberts and Mr. Murray, late a Major in the 10th Hussars. At about half-past 11 o'clock several pistol shots were heard in Mr. Roberts's chambers, after which the back window was thrown open, and Major Murray leaped out into the back yard. He then scaled the wall, and entered the garden of the next house, occupied by Mr. Ransom, who, finding that Major Murray, a stranger to him, was bleeding from the neck and forehead, assisted him to the Charing-cross Hospital, and sent a messenger to the police-office in Scotland-yard, whence constables were sent to examine the premises. In the meantime information was sent from the hospital to the police-station, Bow-street, whereupon Superintendent Durkin and Inspector Mackenzie proceeded to the spot, and undertook the investigation. The doors of the apartments being locked, a ladder was procured, and an entry effected by the windows. In the back room they found traces of a recent struggle. The furniture was disordered, pictures and frames smashed, and great pools of blood were on the floor. Several pistols were found about the room; one pair of which had been discharged. In the front room they found Mr. Roberts, much hurt about the head and face, huddled up against the wall near the door almost insensible. He was removed to the hospital. He has not yet been able to give any account of the transaction. Major Murray states that he knows nothing of Mr. Roberts, and had never seen him till that day, but had been invited by him to his chambers to speak of some pecuniary matters relating to a company with which Major Murray is connected; that Roberts fired upon him twice, and that he defended himself with the firetongs until he had disabled Roberts. Major Murray is not so much injured but that hopes may be entertained of his recovery. Both now lie in the hospital under the care of Dr. Canton, and are guarded by the police.

About 1 o'clock in the afternoon Superintendent Durkin waited on Mr. Corrie, the sitting magistrate at the Bow-street Police-court, and made a communication, in consequence of which Mr. Corrie, accompanied by Mr. Burnaby, the chief clerk, proceeded to the Charing-cross Hospital to take the deposition of Major Murray. Dr. Canton, however, informed his worship that the patient was not in a position to make any deposition, being at that time unable to articulate. He had administered a stimulant, and expected that the patient would shortly be well enough to speak again. In consequence of this representation Mr. Corrie abandoned for the present the idea of taking the depositions. Mr. Canton, however, undertook that if Major Murray should appear to be sinking he would communicate with the magistrate, in order that the deposition might be taken.

It appeared that, though the inmates of the house (Northumberland-chambers, 16, Northumberland-street) heard the sound of pistols, they paid no attention to it, as it was no

Deadly Encounters

Two Victorian Sensations

Richard D. Altick

upp

UNIVERSITY OF PENNSYLVANIA PRESS
Philadelphia
1986

Copyright © 1986 by the University of Pennsylvania Press

Library of Congress Cataloging-in-Publication Data

Altick, Richard Daniel, 1915–
  Deadly encounters.

  Includes index.
    1. Murder—England—London—History—19th century—
Case studies.   2. Crime and criminals in mass media—
England—London—History—19th century—Case studies.
I. Title.
HV6535.G6L615   1986   364.1′523′09421   86-1511
ISBN 0-8122-8011-3 (alk. paper)
ISBN 0-8122-1227-4 (pbk: alk. paper)

Printed in the United States of America

CONTENTS

PREFACE

In this double-feature account of the mysterious and bloody indoor battle in Northumberland Street and Baron de Vidil's unexplained assault on his son in a Twickenham lane, I have invented no detail, however insignificant. Any deviation from the strict truth may be laid to the momentary inaccuracy or imaginative indulgence found in the day-by-day newspaper reportage on which my narrative is wholly based, thanks to the resources of that splendid institution for the preservation of the historic moment, the British Library's Newspaper Library at Colindale.

As for the issues left unresolved—exactly what *was* Mrs. Murray's relationship with William Roberts? just what, if anything, did young Vidil know about his father that he was so anxious not to divulge to the court, and conversely, what damaging statements might his father have made about him if he had been allowed to testify?—the reader has before him all the evidence that, so far as I know, was on the public record in 1861, and his guesses are as good as mine.

R. D. A.

DEADLY ENCOUNTERS

CHAPTER ONE

The Dawning Age of Sensation

Sensation (noun): 3 (a) An exciting experience; a strong emotion (e.g. of terror, hope, curiosity, etc.) aroused by some particular occurrence or situation. Also, in generalized use, the production of violent emotion as an aim in works of literature or art. (b) A condition of excited feeling produced in a community by some occurrence; a strong impression (e.g. of horror, admiration, surprise, etc.) produced in an audience or body of spectators, and manifested by their demeanour.   —*Oxford English Dictionary*

Some applications of the word, at least in England, were new in 1861; the social phenomenon they referred to was not. Sixty years earlier, William Wordsworth, in, of all places, the preface to the second edition of *Lyrical Ballads*, deplored the "craving for extraordinary incident," the "degrading outrageous stimulation" that affected his countrymen. The human desire to be shocked or thrilled, so long as whatever danger there was did not imminently affect the beholder, had always been a normal accompaniment to life in society, perhaps intensified in modern times, as Wordsworth hazarded, by "the accumulation of men in cities" and "the rapid communication of intelligence." Sometimes this fascination with the extraordinary, the perilous, the violent erupted, briefly, into a fever, stirred by a single well-publicized or particularly novel event. But what distinguished the outburst in 1861 was that sensation itself, so to speak, was the sensation. It was a craze that lasted an entire decade, evoking a spate of worried commentaries in the intellectual periodicals and leaving a lasting mark on English fiction and popular drama. Although one cannot say with absolute certainty that a single event ignited the sensation mania of the 1860s, a pair of mysterious, murderous attacks in and near London in the summer of 1861, covered by the energetic press with almost unprecedented thoroughness and excitement, occurred in a gathering atmosphere for which they were providentially suited.

On Saturday, 20 July, just one week after the Murray and Vidil cases first broke in the London press, *Punch* ran a set of lighthearted verses that had obviously been written before those crimes immediately lent a more sinister connotation to the new vogue word:

> Some would have it an age of Sensation,
>   If the age one of Sense may not be—
> The word's not *Old* England's creation,
>   But New England's, over the sea—
> Where all's in the high-pressure way,
>   In life just as in locomotion,
> And where, though you're here for to-day,
>   Where to-morrow you'll be, you've no notion.
>
> In that land of fast life and fast laws—
>   Laws not faster made than they're broken—
> Sensation's the spirit that draws
>   To a head, whate'er's written or spoken.
> If a steamer blow up on the lakes,
>   Or a statesman prove false to the nation,
> Its impression the circumstance makes
>   In a paragraph headed "Sensation."
>
> If a senator gouges a friend
>   In the course of a lively debate;
> Or a pleasure-train comes to an end
>   By trying to leap a lock-gate;
> If the great Hiram Dodge takes the stump,
>   Or the President makes an oration,
> The event able Editors lump
>   Under one standing head of "Sensation."
>
> The last horrid murder down South,
>   The last monster mile-panorama;

Last new sermon, or wash for the mouth,
    New acrobat, planet or drama;
All—all is Sensation—so fast
    Piled up by this go-a-head nation,
That by dint of Sensation at last,
    There's nothing excites a "Sensation."

And now that across the Atlantic
    Worn threadbare "Sensation" we've seen,
And the people that lately were frantic,
    Blush to think that such madmen they've been;
Mr. Punch sees with pain and surprise,
    On the part of this common sense nation,
Every here and there, on the rise,
    This pois'nous exotic "Sensation."

When an acrobat ventures his neck,
    In the feats of the flying trapeze,
Or some nigger minstrel would deck
    His wool-wig with extra green bays;
If a drama can boast of a run,
    By dint of a strong situation,
The posters e'en now have begun
    To puff the thing up as "Sensation."

Mr. Punch 'gainst the word and the things
    It applies to, his protest would enter:
For the vulgar excitement it brings
    May England ne'er prove fitting centre.
If you've got something good, never doubt it
    By deeds will avouch its vocation;
And be sure that not talking about it
    Is the true way to *make* a "Sensation."

The United States had no monopoly on railroad wrecks, steamship explosions, political melodrama, or daredevils: the stuff of sensation was as abundant in Britain as in America. To be sure, some of the most exciting events and persons in the English newspapers in the past two decades had been American importations. P. T. Barnum's winsome midget, General Tom Thumb, had been the adored star of the nation's entertainment world in the 1840s, closely followed by George Catlin's troupe of Red Indians. The visit of Harriet Beecher Stowe, author of *Uncle Tom's Cabin*, a book that broke all best-seller records in Britain in 1851, took the form of a royal progress, marked by almost hysterical outpourings of adulation. "Monster mile-panoramas"— visual travelogues, the first being of a trip down the Mississippi, embodied in painted lengths of canvas that unrolled before a rapt audience—had been a popular and profitable novelty in English theaters.

What had, up to this point, distinguished the British sensations from their American counterparts was that the former had not yet been given that name, which had originated in an American press that, as Dickens and other travelers had noted, was uninhibited by any considerations of decorum or discretion. Their eyes steadily fixed on a readership that craved constant shocks and thrills, American newspapers were in the habit of "sensationalizing" any events that even faintly lent themselves to such treatment. The same was true of publicity, not only for theatrical and other forms of entertainment but for some kinds of consumer goods, largely nonessential items. Today's word to cover all of this would be simply "hype."

Although *Punch* deplored journalistic and commercial sensationalism as a Yankee abomination to be firmly barred from sedate, low-key Britain, there was a strong native strain of the same malady. Until recently, the daily press had been relatively sober, though thorough, in its coverage of domestic news; the Sunday papers, however, like the mass circulation ones in today's London, specialized in vividly written stories of violence and scandal, particularly such as occurred, or were said to occur, in the higher reaches of society. The generally radical politics of such sheets as *Reynolds' Weekly Newspaper* and *Lloyd's Weekly Newspaper* harmonized well with news columns calculated to stir the cruder feelings of their working-class and lower-middle-class readers. The London daily press took on a more "popular" tone, with no scanting of quantity, when the abolition of the old newspaper tax in 1855 enabled the *Daily Telegraph* to become the first penny daily in British history. And as far as commercial publicity was concerned, London had its own brand of hype in the specially built wagons, some bearing hugely enlarged imitations of the products advertised (a seven-foot hat, for example) that clogged traffic in central London, and the corps of sandwich board men who likewise clogged the sidewalks in behalf of current entertainments and products.

Although it occupied only an incidental place in *Punch*'s list of American sensations, murder was a staple of the English entertainment diet. It had long been so, as the survival of countless broadsides, ballads, "last dying speeches," and catchpenny pamphlets for the delectation of the populace, attests, as does the popularity, on a higher social level, of the several nineteenth-century editions of the *Newgate Calendar*, a compendium of accounts of famous murder trials. Now, however, a formidably expanding daily press had acquired the capacity to spread news of the latest homicides to the remotest part of the British Isles within hours. The previous half-dozen years had witnessed a series of well-publicized murders that were distinguished from the ordinary run of contemporaneous homicides by their occurrence in middle-class families, a realm of Victorian society that had always been assumed to be exempt from such catastrophes by virtue of its much-vaunted "respectability." In 1856, after a trial to which the press gave the heaviest coverage to date, a Staffordshire physician named William Palmer was convicted of poisoning six people, including one of his illegitimate children, his mother-in-law, his alcoholic brother, and his wife. The next year, Madeleine Smith, the pretty and spirited daughter of a prosperous Edinburgh architect, stood trial for poisoning her French lover with hot chocolate laced with arsenic; she was neither convicted nor acquitted, the jury rendering the ambiguous Scottish verdict of "not proven." In 1859, another physician, Thomas Smethurst, was tried for allegedly murdering a woman to whom he was bigamously married. He was convicted, but, largely because the circumstantial and scientific case against him was palpably inadequate, he was granted a pardon. Scarcely had the furor over Smethurst subsided than Constance Kent, the sixteen-year-old daughter of a government factory inspector, was accused of killing her four-year-old step-brother at their home at Road, Wiltshire. Despite the strong case against her made by a Scotland Yard detective who had been called in after the local constabulary found themselves hopelessly out of their depth, the magistrates before whom she was arraigned set her free; upon which Inspector Whicher resigned from the force. The question of Constance's guilt or innocence continued to be debated as 1861 began. (She confessed to the deed five years later, but this did little to resolve the question even then. In 1868, Wilkie Collins would take advantage of the still lively memories of the Road mystery, as it was called, by using several of its features in *The Moonstone*.)

Three major news stories in the first half of 1861 qualified as sensations, although the word was not used as yet outside the theater. The first (21 February–8 March) was the trial, in Dublin, of *Thelwall* v. *Yelverton*. At first glance it was the most prosaic of actions, merely that of a tradesman suing a man for £259 he owed for goods supplied to his wife; but the crucial question of law was whether they were in fact married. Theresa Longworth, daughter of a Manchester silk merchant and descendant of an ancient family, had become the object of the attentions of Major Yelverton, second son of Lord Avonmore, who pursued her all the way across Europe to the Crimea, where he was serving with the army and she was doing nursing service as a vowless Sister of Charity. Upon their return to England in 1857, with her consent they went through a form of do-it-yourself ("Scotch") marriage, whereby the private reading of the Anglican marriage service was sufficient to unite bride and groom. The lady, however, held out in addition for a Roman Catholic service, which was performed secretly some days later by a complaisant priest. But the following year, having left his Theresa, the major married another woman, the widow of an Edinburgh professor. Was this a bigamous marriage, or had either or both of the preceding ceremonies been without legal standing?

The dry point of law was eclipsed by the dramatic testimony, the star witness being the vivacious, intelligent, "ladylike" young woman who insisted on calling herself "Mrs. Yelverton." Day after day, newspaper readers were regaled with "the strange revelations of life incident to the Crimean campaign—the beauty, talent, and ill-regulated passions of the victim—the conventional moral maxims of the seducer and the phantasmagoric manner in which foreign convents, Sisters of Charity, Greek priests, priestless Scotch marriages, and Roman Catholic priests, came and went." Newspapers even sacrificed their leading articles (editorials) and advertising space to provide maximum coverage, which was strongly biased in favor of the imprudent but victimized woman. When the jury decided that both the Scotch and the Roman Catholic marriages were valid in law, "the whole audience rose and cheered tumultuously, the ladies waving their handkerchiefs, the gentlemen their hats, and the barristers their wigs."

The Yelverton case was rich in titillation. The major, for example, described spending one memorable afternoon with the temporary-duty Sister of Charity in a room at the Crimean hospital, where he "formed—not the 'design,' that was too strong a word, not the 'desire,' that was too strong a word, but the 'idea' of making her his mistress." But persons who preferred other kinds of vicarious excitement had to look elsewhere, and on the first of June they were obliged. On that day, the French acrobat Blondin made his first appearance at the Crystal Palace, the spacious entertainment center in the south London suburb of Sydenham, which had been built with the materials salvaged from the iron-and-glass structure that housed the Great Exhibition in Hyde Park in 1851. Blondin, a former infant prodigy who had taken to the air at the age of four, was, in a sense, another American importation, for he had most recently been in the news as the man who the previous year had walked a tightrope across the 1,200-foot chasm of Niagara Falls. During his summer engagement at the Crystal Palace he worked on an inch-and-a-half-thick rope suspended 180 feet above the central transept. One highlight of his performance before sellout crowds was walking blindfolded with a sack over his head, then standing on his head and doing a backward somersault. In another act, he took a fifty-pound stove with him onto the rope, lighted a fire, cooked an omelette, and served himself with dishes on a tray, topping the aerial repast with a bottle of wine. Only a newly enlisted word like "sensation" was adequate to describe such a series of feats.

Three weeks after Blondin's Crystal Palace debut, on Saturday, 22 June, a sprawling complex of wharves and warehouses between the Thames and Tooley Street, opposite the City, caught fire. The crowds that watched from London Bridge were as large as those that had witnessed from Westminster Bridge the destruction of the old Houses of Parliament in 1834. By the time the fire was finally brought under control—Dickens saw it still "blazing furiously" a week later—it had devastated a quarter-mile of Bermondsey waterfront and caused the then stupendous loss of £2 million in buildings and their contents. The chief of the London Fire Brigade, James Braidwood, was killed in action. It is curious to reflect that just three weeks later, on Friday, 12 July, Major Murray would have seen the still smoldering ruins as he changed from his train at London Bridge to the riverboat that would carry him to his fateful encounter with "Mr. Gray" in Hungerford Market.

Meanwhile, from mid-April onward, the outbreak of the American Civil War commanded much space in the press; but though the dispatches from Washington and Charleston were interesting enough, they could be read with placid detachment. President Lincoln's call to preserve the Union and the blockade of Confederate ports, events occurring thousands of miles away, had no immediate pertinence either to the affairs of empire or to everyday life in Britain.

For readers whose appetites ran to murder above all, it was a lean six months. Late in August, a newspaper reviewing the furor over the Murray and Vidil cases commented that until they had commenced their run in the press "public attention . . . had seemed palled into incurable lethargy by the Barmecide feast of less romantic atrocities that had been preceding them." On 13 July the weekly *Spectator* reported that apart from a number of commonplace murders, "the week has been a dull one, distinguished socially only by the celebration of the Queen's birthday, which occurs whenever Her Majesty pleases, and was this year fixed for 10th July, and by the meeting of the National Rifle Association at Wimbledon." Had the *Spectator* but known it, the doldrums were suddenly at an end. Elsewhere in its pages was a brief mention of the Vidil case, picked up from the preceding day's *Morning Post*. But nowhere did it mention the other stop-press affair that the morning papers piled alongside it at London newsagents' were featuring in adjacent columns. Between them, in the weeks to come, the unfolding stories of the blood bath in a Northumberland Street office and the brutal assault of father upon son that had occurred earlier in a secluded Surrey lane would usher in what soon came to be called the Age of Sensation.

CHAPTER TWO

Deadly Encounters

FRIDAY, 12 JULY
(Murray)

The next morning's newspapers carried the "unaccountable" confrontation as their main story. The British press had not yet gone in for banner headlines, but its single-column captions made up in concerted drama what they lacked in size. They drew from a common, though limited, fount of sensational epithets. TERRIBLE TRAGEDY IN THE STRAND, shouted the *Daily Telegraph*. MURDEROUS ENCOUNTER IN NORTHUMBERLAND STREET, echoed the *Morning Post*. FRIGHTFUL ENCOUNTER IN NORTHUMBERLAND STREET, cried the *Times*. DEADLY ENCOUNTER IN NORTHUMBERLAND STREET, FEARFUL STRUGGLE FOR LIFE, added the *Morning Chronicle*. EXTRAORDINARY AND DESPERATE AFFRAY IN THE STRAND was the *Daily News*'s variation on the universal theme.

Before we look into the particulars of the occurrence that evoked this spate of lurid headlines, we must pinpoint its location, which to the public was so important an aspect of the case that every headline featured it, immediately lending to the event the name by which it was to be remembered, "the Northumberland Street affair." That two of the papers specified the Strand rather than the more accurate Northumberland Street merely indicates that, like London news placards today, they were taking advantage of the customary extension of a well-known place name to cover the whole vicinity. Everyone knew where the Strand was; it was the busiest street in the West End with

Front View of the House in Northumberland Street

The Rear of the House in Northumberland Street

its shops and offices, thronged sidewalks, and heavy traffic going to and from the City. Leading down from it to the Thames, between Hungerford Market and Northumberland House, the last private estate to survive in central London (it would be razed in 1874 to make way for the present Northumberland Avenue, a broad thoroughfare leading from Trafalgar Square to the Victoria Embankment), were two narrow streets, Craven and Northumberland. These were connected halfway down by a short byway called Craven Passage or Court.

For many years the neighborhood had enjoyed a fashionable reputation. Northumberland Street was lined with brick houses built in the plain style popular after the Great Fire.* Many doorways were of elegant design, and some of the interiors were distinguished by turned stair-railings, paneling, and decorated ceilings. Now, however, most of the householding population had dispersed elsewhere, and many of the premises were given over to company offices, the rooms of professional persons such as civil engineers, and boarding and lodging houses. Number 16, which the newspapers described as dingy-looking, with "neglected" windows and blinds, was near the bottom of the street, and thus, notwithstanding the early headlines, at some distance from the Strand. It and the houses on either side were collectively known as Northumberland Chambers, owned by the Catalonia Cork-Cutting Company, whose workshop and office occupied Number 17.

Between eleven-thirty and noon on Friday, one Thomas Clay, the foreman of the company, and a workman named William Clark were repairing the water cistern in the yard of Number 16. From the rear first (American: second) floor room, which overlooked the yard, came the sound of firearms being discharged. As Clay was to testify ten days later, this caused no particular surprise, because he had heard similar reports coming from the room on earlier occasions. After about five minutes, there was another burst, and still Clay and Clark went about their business. Evidently the sound of indoor gunfire was not uncommon, even in the heart of commercial London. Another five minutes passed, and this time the men were forced to recognize that something truly out of the ordinary was taking place. One of the frosted first-floor windows was raised, and a well-dressed gentle-

---

* At the foot of the street was the outflow of a main sewer, from which, if the tide was right, the effluent crossed the Thames to be pumped into the intake of the Lambeth water supply—a quintessentially Victorian touch.

man with a fair complexion and dark whiskers, his face covered with blood, thrust his leg over the sill as if about to jump.

"Good God, what's the matter?" cried Clay.

"There has been murder done here," replied the man.

"For God's sake," Clay said, "don't come out of the window, you'll kill yourself. I'll come up." Sending Clark for the police, Clay went into the house and up to the two-room suite occupied by a bill discounter and moneylender named Roberts. (The initial reports said, mistakenly, that he was also a solicitor. Other inaccuracies in the first stories will be silently corrected in the light of later information.) Each room had a door giving onto the staircase, but both were locked. Clay then went upstairs to the second-floor office of Preston Lumb, a civil engineer, and was about to bring down with him the managing clerk, Henry Ransom, when from the yard they heard the sound of smashing glass. He therefore ran downstairs and into the yard, to find the man he had seen at the window vaulting the low wall that separated the yard from that of the adjoining house, Number 15. The fugitive, it later transpired, had tried first to descend by a drainpipe leading from the inside water closet, but this angled away too sharply for him to slide down, and so, clinging to the windowsill, he had managed to place his feet on the top frame of one of the ground-floor windows and then jumped, barely avoiding a further fall into the areaway outside the basement. He landed instead on two wicker baskets containing water filters, one of which he broke. As he descended he had kicked out panes of glass from the ground-floor windows, which accounted for the noise that brought Clay into the yard. Left behind in the yard were his umbrella and a fragment of a fire tongs covered with blood and hair. Clay grabbed at the fugitive's coat tails as he went over the wall, but he shook himself loose and disappeared into the corridor of Number 15. Clay then went into the corresponding hallway of Number 16 and, in the only farcical moment in what was rapidly becoming a serious incident indeed, fugitive and pursuer collided as they emerged at the respective front doors on Northumberland Street.

Meanwhile, the workman Clark had touched off a hue and cry, perhaps by going to the office of his employer, the Catalonia Cork-Cutting Company, on the ground floor of Number 17; at least, the first newspaper reports said it was a man named Pomfret, later identified as an official of the company, who first raised the cry of "Murder!" Clark and Ransom together tried to break into the rear room on the

Thomas Clay

Henry Ransom

first floor. It then occurred to Ransom that it would be imprudent to do so. "What blockheads we are to try and force the door!" he exclaimed to Clark. "If a man has been murdered, the other man may be behind the door, and may shoot us."

Thereupon they went downstairs and found the mysterious man from the window standing with Clay on the steps of Number 16. At this point, if not a minute or so earlier, the first policeman arrived on the scene, Sergeant Golden, badge 46A, who according to his later testimony had been passing on the opposite side of the street at the moment the alarm was raised. He sent at once for his superiors, Superintendent Durkin of Scotland Yard and Inspector Mackenzie of F Division, headquartered in Bow Street.

A closer inspection of the man whom Clark, Clay, and Ransom detained revealed that in addition to his blood-covered face, his hair and whiskers were singed and burned, and it now appeared also that he had a wound in the back of the neck from which blood was copiously flowing. Ransom asked him to come in and sit down. "No," said the man, "not where I have been attempted to be murdered. Give me my umbrella, and let me go to my office."

"No, you cannot," said Ransom. "You must have medical aid."

"Am I wounded?" asked the man.

Superintendent Durkin and Inspector MacKenzie, the Police Officials in Charge of the Northumberland Street Investigation

"Yes, fearfully wounded," Ransom replied.

"Had I two pistols," said the man, "I would have shot him also."

When Ransom observed that "the man who has done it may escape," the wounded one said with unmistakable relish, "I have served him out for this too much for him to make his escape."

Sergeant Golden then handed him over to Ransom, advising him to find a doctor. While they waited for Clay to retrieve the umbrella from the yard, the man identified himself as Major Murray, late of the Tenth Hussars.* (One of the minor peculiarities of the affair was that he did not give his Christian name even to the surgeon attending him, and that it was never mentioned in the press until the last day of the

---

*One of the few writers on the case, Sir John Hall, collected information on the major's military career. which did not figure in the legal proceedings. Born in 1819, the son of a Jamaican planter, he bought a cornetry in the Tenth Hussars in 1838, was promoted to lieutenant two years later, and served with the regiment in India from 1845. The regiment fought in the Crimea, but although Murray asserted in his testimony that he had served there, the Army List does not show that he received the Crimea medal. Seniority, if nothing else, won him promotion to the rank of brevet major. In May 1857 he exchanged into the Lancers but sold his commission before the end of the year.

inquest.) He was, he said, a director of the Grosvenor Hotel Company with offices at 25 Parliament Street. The Grosvenor, brand new at the time, still stands and flourishes adjacent to Victoria Station. It has a double interest, to students of mid-Victorian architecture especially for its application of John Ruskin's pattern of "the oak, the ivy, and the rose" to its cornice friezes, and to students of crime as a conspicuous if fortuitous memento of one of its original shareholders. Murray added that he resided with his mother and brother at 33 Harley Street, Cavendish Square. "That damned fellow upstairs has shot me, by the name of Gray," said the major. Ransom said that nobody by that name occupied the chambers above. "Yes, there is," the major insisted; "he gave me the name of Gray." Ransom then asked him if it was the same gentleman with whom he, Ransom, had earlier seen him coming down Craven Court toward Northumberland Street—a short gentleman, dressed in black. "Yes, that is the fellow," the major replied. Ransom said that that gentleman's name was Roberts.

(Because the confusion of names was an integral part of the mystery as it first developed, the press took pains to establish just who the tenants of Number 16 were. Inscribed on brass plates or painted alongside the door were the names of "Nicholson & Co.," "The London and West-end Mercantile Agency," "Roberts," and "Walker.")

The major having got his umbrella back, the two men set out in search of medical aid, and an arresting sight they must have been in the midst of London at noon on a summer day—a soberly dressed senior clerk and an exemplar of the walking wounded, a man whose blood, flowing from temple and neck, had soaked his coat and shirt. As they walked through Craven Court they met Police Constable Arber, 155F, to whom the major said, "Go round to No. 16 Northumberland Street, for a man has shot me in the neck; he is in the first floor." Constable Arber, evidently assured that the bloody gentleman with the umbrella was in reliable hands, hastened to the scene, and the two resumed their stroll. They stopped in at a chemist's, but, convinced by one glance that the major required more than superficial first aid, the shopkeeper recommended that they proceed to the nearby Charing Cross Hospital.

It was at this time that Murray told Ransom the story which he repeated, with some amplification, at the inquest ten days later.* He had come down by penny boat from London Bridge to Hungerford

*In the interest of providing a full narrative of the Homeric encounter at the outset, I have taken the liberty of enlarging the major's first compressed account by adding

Stairs—these were the days when transport by river was cheaper and faster than by cab or omnibus through the traffic-choked London streets—and walked through Hungerford Market, already marked for demolition as the site of the Charing Cross Station. As he headed for the Strand, he was accosted by a stranger who lifted his hat and asked, "Have I the pleasure of addressing Major Murray?"

"I said, 'Yes, that's my name;' and he then said, 'I believe you are a director of the Grosvenor Hotel Company?' I said, 'Yes, I am; and pray who are you?' He said, 'My name is Gray.' I had never seen him before in my life. I said, 'How do you know me?' and Gray replied, 'I have seen you at the meetings of the company.' I said, 'Are you a shareholder?' He said, 'No, but I attended the meetings.'

"He then went on to say he had a client who had £60,000, and he understood the Company wanted to borrow money, and his client was anxious to get the investment. I said I had no power in the matter, as I was only one of ten directors, and could do nothing personally; but I added, 'If you will give me your name and address, I am going to the Company, and will say what you wish.' He said that would do, and that, if not in a hurry, he would like me to come to his office and answer a few questions. I asked where his office was and he said close round the corner.

"By this time we were at the door of his office, and he asked me to step upstairs. He showed me into a back room on the first floor, and requested me to be seated. I never was in the house before—most positively, never. I took a seat; and he then said, 'You will excuse me for one instant,' and left the room. I sat with my back to the folding doors in front of the table. On my left was the fireplace. The folding doors were shut. When he left the room I took a look round, and thought it was the most extraordinary place I had ever seen; torn papers, bottles, and pictures lying about: a most disreputable-looking place.

"In a minute or so he came back into the room and took a seat in front of me, with a pen in his hand, and asked what interest we proposed to give. I said I was not in a position to say, but would hear what his client proposed to ask. He said, 'Oh, then, I understand the offer is to come from us.' I said not, as under any circumstances we should not give more than five per cent. He replied, 'That will do very well;'

---

details he subsequently supplied to the police and the coroner's jury. This version is based on the one the *Annual Register* for the year synthesized from the various newspaper reports.

and I asked him for his card of address. He said, 'Immediately,' and got up from the table and walked round behind me and began rummaging among the papers on a desk. I thought he was looking for his card, and took no particular notice.

"Presently, I felt a touch in the back of my neck. There was a report of a pistol, and I dropped off the chair on the ground. I was perfectly paralyzed. I could not move any part of my body. My head, however, was quite clear. I was lying with my face to the fender, and when he fired I believe he left the room. After some little time I felt returning life in my leg and arm, and I was just raising myself on my elbow when I heard a door open, and he came in again. He immediately walked up behind me and fired a pistol into my right temple. I dropped back on the carpet, and the blood gushed all over my face, and eyes, and mouth, in a regular torrent. He either stooped or knelt down close behind me, for I could feel his breath, and he watched close to see if I was dead.

"I then made up my mind to pretend to be so. I felt that the bleeding was bringing life back to me fast all over my body, which was tingling to the fingers' ends. I knew if I could get on to my feet I should be able to make a fight for it. After he had knelt behind me for some short time he got up and walked away, and I then opened my eyes and took a look round, and saw a pair of tongs within a few inches of my hand. Feeling that my strength was returning to me, and there was the whole length of the room between us, I seized the tongs, and sprang to my feet. He was then at the window. Hearing me move, he turned and faced me. I at once rushed at him, and made a heavy blow at him with the tongs, which missed. I then seized them short by the middle, and made a dash into his chest and face, which knocked him over on his back. I got my knees on his chest, and tried to smash his head with the tongs. They were too long, and he got them in both his hands firmly.

"I struggled hard for some time to get them away, but he was as strong as I, and I could not do it. I looked round for something else to hit him with, and close to my right hand I saw a large black bottle, which I caught in my right hand, and shaking the tongs with my left, to keep him occupied, I hit him full, with all my force, on the middle of the forehead, and smashed it to pieces. That made him like quiver all over, but still he did not let go the tongs, so I caught hold of a metal vase and dashed it at his head with all my might, but I missed him. Then, as I saw there was nothing else at hand, I set to work desperately to get the mastery of the tongs, which he was holding all the time. During all this he was on his back, close under the window nearest the door.

"After a long struggle I got the tongs. As they came into my hands I lost my balance, and fell back, but was up again in an instant, and by that time he was rising into a sitting position, which gave me a fair, full blow at his head with the tongs, and I gave it him with all my might and main. I repeated it three or four times. He hid his head under the table to escape my blows, and I then hit him over the back of the neck; and in order to disable his hands, I hit him hard over the wrists.

"I then thought he was sufficiently disabled and tried to get out, but the door of the room was locked. I then went through the folding doors of the front room and tried that way, but that door was locked too. In coming back through the folding doors, I met him again face to face, walking towards me. I took a step back in order to get a full swing, and hit him on the head again with the tongs. He fell forward on his face through the folding doors as if he was dead. I pushed his feet through the doors and shut them, and then threw up the window."

By this time they had arrived at Charing Cross Hospital. The house surgeon determined that the major was suffering from two wounds, a superficial one in front of the right ear and a much more serious one that began with a jagged opening below the right mastoid process and extended to the spine, where a bullet was embedded. Because of the length and contracted state of the path it had taken, he had great difficulty in dislodging it, but eventually he succeeded (the ball proved to be indented with the mark of the vertebra against which it rested), and the patient was given what was variously described as a "restorative" or "stimulant" and placed in bed.

Back in Northumberland Street, renewed attempts were being made to enter the locked rooms. After Sergeant Golden delivered Major Murray into the care of Henry Ransom, he went upstairs, along with Thomas Clay and a young man who identified himself as Roberts's son. The youth acted, he said, as a clerk and writ server for his father and a solicitor named John Francis Walker, who occupied an office on the first floor of the adjoining house, Number 17, which communicated with Number 16 on that level. The key was on the outside of the rear room door, but the room was locked from the inside. At that point they were joined by Superintendent Durkin, Inspector Mackenzie, Constable Arber, and a fresh recruit, Constable Langley. When the door refused to yield to the force of sheer numbers, Clay

"Close to My Right Hand I Saw a Large Black Bottle, Which I Caught in My Right Hand, and Shaking the Tongs with My Left, to Keep Him Occupied, I Hit Him Full, with All My Force, on the Middle of the Forehead." (From a contemporary print.)

sent Clark to fetch a ladder into the yard. Constable Arber climbed it to enter the room by the route Murray had employed in his precipitate escape, and unlocking the door, he admitted his fellow officers, Clay, and young Roberts.

They were appalled by the sight presented by the room, where the smell and smoke of gunpowder still lingered despite the opened rear window. But where was the man who had engaged Major Murray in a murderous struggle? There was no sign of him, and they did not know as yet what the major had told Ransom, that he had, in Hamlet's expressive phrase, lugged the guts into the neighbor room. But there was only one other place to look for him, and, opening the folding doors to the other room, they found him huddled in a corner: William James Roberts, aged forty-five. His face and head were a mass of pulp, and he bled from no fewer than thirteen separate lacerations, the worst of which was eight and one-half inches long. His eyelids were swollen shut, and, as the medical men later discovered, several bones in his skull were shattered. "How did this happen?" asked one of the policemen. "Done by that man gone downstairs," answered Roberts with obvious difficulty. Arber and Langley carried him into the rear room, covered his face with a cloth, and sent for a cab. Roberts resisted their help. "Let me sit down here and die," he pleaded. But the cab came, and he was delivered to the hospital shortly after Murray and Ransom arrived under their own power.

The policemen, led by Superintendent Durkin and Inspector Mackenzie, now searched both rooms. Although the description the *Times* printed on the following Tuesday was denounced by more than one rival paper as being too highly colored, its tone epitomizes the spirit of morbid wonder with which the public watched this bizarre case unfold. Perhaps the furnishings of Roberts's rooms were not what the *Times* implied, a rich treasure a connoisseur might have bought with the proceeds from Ali Baba's cave. That they might have been only a miscellaneous assortment of pledges accumulated by a money-lender in the ordinary course of business detracted little from the romantic glamour the scene had for press and public alike. Readers of current fiction might envision it as the real-life counterpart of the never aired, never dusted room in which Miss Havisham, the disappointed bride still clad in her wedding finery, secluded herself in Dickens's *Great Expectations*, then about to conclude its serial run in his weekly paper, *All the Year Round*. Others might have linked the room with another premarital casualty, "Dirty Dick" (Nathaniel Bentley), an innkeeper in eighteenth-century Bishopsgate, who, after his bride-to-

"There Was Only One Other Place to Look for Roberts, and, Opening the Folding Doors to the Front Room, the Policemen Found Him Huddled in a Corner." (From a contemporary print.)

be died on the eve of their wedding feast, had lived out his long life in penury and cobwebbed squalor, becoming part of London legend and doubtless inspiring Dickens as he portrayed the grim stasis of Miss Havisham's Satis House.

A description of these rooms [said the *Times*] would read almost like a chapter from a French novel. The front room has originally been furnished in the most luxurious and costly style. On the walls are five watercolour drawings, and between them handsome brackets, supporting statuettes and copies from the antique. Round the room are ranged costly buhl cabinets and inlaid tables, on which are all sorts of ornaments under large glass shades. It is not, however, until one has been in the room some time that the richness of the furniture attracts notice, for glasses, pictures, statuettes, and vases—even the very cabinets themselves, are almost concealed under the accumulated dust of years. The shades and ornaments are enveloped in this as if coated with a positive fur, and even the slightly relieved figures which are on a copy of the Portland vase that stands on a sideboard in a corner are barely distinguishable under their fine black coating. In spite of the costliness of its furniture, and the taste that has been bestowed upon its arrangement in the room, it is evident that it has never been cleaned or dusted probably since the things were first placed there many years ago. In the centre of the room is the table at which Mr. Roberts used to work, with the fire-place on the right hand, having an exceedingly handsome white marble mantelpiece, which is marked with bullets. Yet, almost immediately under the mantelpiece, making a great mound that stretches out into the centre of the floor, are the waste papers which have been crumpled up and thrown aside, and allowed, like the dust, to accumulate undisturbed. It appears to have been the habit of Mr. Roberts to allow no one but himself to enter his room, and thus the papers and the dust and dirt have collected till the former half fill the front room and the latter obscure the contents of both. Except an overturned chair, and papers scattered about, there is very little sign of a struggle in this room.

The condition of the rear room lent instant credibility to the blow-by-blow narrative Ransom had heard from Major Murray.

The back drawing-room [continued the *Times*] was as richly furnished and as dirty as the front. But the dust has here been beaten down and the gloomy richness of the room disturbed by the most desperate of all contests—a contest where strong and angry men struggle to tear and beat each other down with whatever weapon they can seize in their frenzy. If two wild beasts had been turned loose to kill each other in this apartment it could not have presented traces of a more prolonged or deadly contest than it does. The furniture is broken and overturned in hideous confusion; the walls, the gilded tables, backs of chairs, and sides of dirty inlaid cabinets are streaked and smeared about with bloody fingers. One may almost trace where blows were struck by the star-shaped splashes of blood along the walls, while over the glass shades of the ornaments and doors of the cabinets it has fallen like rain, as if a bloody mop had been trundled round and round there.

The *Times*'s breathless survey of the scene went on and on. Vivid journalism outdid itself as it rejected a cliché, long familiar in descriptions of routine cases of mayhem, that it justly deemed not only inaccurate but inadequate for this occasion: "There were no pools of blood, as they are called, for blood neither sinks into the carpet nor flows away, but there were in many places lumps of thick gore nearly half an inch high, and showing clearly that each had flowed from the wounds of someone lying immediately over the actual spot." The lavish distribution of bloodstains over the walls, especially near the escape window, clearly mesmerized the reporter, to the extent of repeating his rainstorm metaphor later in the article.

The police inventory of the damage in the rear room was more matter-of-fact but no less impressive: an ormolu writing desk, its baize-covered top wrenched from its frame, its drawers ransacked and one smashed to atoms; a glass case, with a bronze statuette of St. George and the dragon, tipped over; the remaining portion of the fire tongs, broken into half a dozen pieces, to which a man's hairs adhered; two broken bottles and an intact one, all three bearing marks testifying to the ferocity with which they had been employed as weapons (whether they were wine or beer bottles was not firmly established, but either way, they had been fearfully effective as cutting agents and bludgeons); a chair, its back wrenched from the seat; on the floor, four bullets and a brace of horse pistols, neither of which had been recently discharged; on a table, a pair of small, dainty ivory-handled pistols, which had. On the walls were framed chromolithographs, sprinkled with blood; another picture, a portrait of Lord

Nelson, lay shattered on the floor; it too bore hairs of a man's whiskers. On the mantelpiece, surrounded with six holes, lay a dozen flattened bullets. For readers who had not yet "supped full with horrors"—a phrase that was to flow repeatedly from journalists' pens—the *Morning Chronicle* summed up the effect through a heightened selection of details:

> In parts fragments of the usurer's scalp seemed to have flown from his head under the blows of Major Murray's pair of tongs, and adhered to the paper hangings; in one spot a stream of wine had soaked into a mass of gore; in another the maddened belligerents seemed to have writhed together with glass, buhl, books, ornaments, and beer bottles crushing and staining them, while the one, with almost supernatural animosity, was endeavouring to master the other.

"The sooner a photograph is taken of the condition of the apartments," said the *Morning Post* on Monday morning, "the better for the ends of justice." No photograph, at so early a stage in the development of the art, could have done justice to the *Times*'s (and other papers') description, nor could it have been directly reproduced in the press, since a drawing would have had to be made of it for a wood engraver to copy. But one wonders whether a picture was in fact taken of the scene and whether, by any improbable stroke of luck, it still exists somewhere.

At the hospital, Major Murray remained fully conscious and repeated, coherently, faithfully, and with added detail, the story he had told Ransom. Since the medical men were confident that his life was in no danger, the Bow Street magistrate, Mr. Corrie, deferred questioning him. Roberts was in no condition to say anything. That evening, his wife visited him. According to the newspapers (this was another reported detail upon which doubt was later cast), both antagonists had been placed in the same room when they were first admitted to the hospital. Mrs. Roberts turned from her husband's bedside and demanded of Murray, "Why is not Mrs. Murray sent for, as she perhaps may be able to give us some explanation of this?" Murray retorted that she was as mad as her husband. Subsequently, she elaborated to a reporter for the *Morning Post*, saying that, in his words, "a lady, passing by the name of Murray, had been in the habit of calling upon her husband at his office in Northumberland Street, ostensibly on business matters. The visits of this lady," he continued, "whoever she may turn out to be (it is certain she is not Major Murray's wife) were so frequent that they excited the astonishment of Mrs. Roberts, who on more than one occasion inquired of Mr. Roberts how it was that Major Murray did not himself call instead of entrusting his business to a female, but she never got from him a satisfactory explanation."

But no explanation was forthcoming now from her horribly wounded husband, and the mystery—a whole cluster of mysteries—remained. What had been the issue between the two men that had erupted into a life-and-death fight in the rear room of 16 Northumberland Street? Which had been the assailant, and which the intended victim? Was it humanly possible to credit the major's story that he and Roberts had been perfect strangers until he was lured—was he?—to the premises? "Preposterous," said the *Daily Telegraph*. "Utterly incredible," said the *Morning Post*. "Utterly incomprehensible," said the *Times*. The *Morning Chronicle* declared that "we absolutely disbelieve" Murray's fantastic tale, filled as it was with "amazing improbabilities."

The uninhibited freedom the Victorian journalist enjoyed to comment on criminal cases both before and after they became formal legal actions astonishes anyone familiar with the strict constraints that present-day British law imposes on the press in cases *sub judice*. Trial by newspaper was a fact of Victorian life. The press could speculate, report rumors, assess character, decide guilt untrameled by law or any canon of journalistic ethics, and at the same time piously assert its single-minded devotion to truth and justice. The *Daily Telegraph's* Monday editorial was a case in point. In obedience to its conviction that "it is our duty and our determination to eliminate, if possible, the truth from a mass of confusion and contradiction" (in the next column it gave Roberts the wrong Christian names and asserted, wrongly, that he and Murray had walked across Hungerford Bridge together) it fired off a whole fusillade of questions. If Roberts had really meant to kill Murray, why had he used "two delicate little ivory-handled gewgaws" instead of the large pistols he had at hand? How could Murray, with a bullet in the cervical vertebrae, have managed to batter in Roberts's head, sever his temporal artery, and break one of his fingers, shattering a pair of fire tongs in the process? Why did he not cry for assistance from the men in the yard below as Roberts attacked him? Why did he drag Roberts's limp body by the legs into the front room? And so forth. The writer's conclusion, that "we have very little faith in the statement made by Major Murray," was one of the few understatements printed in the course of news coverage, which throughout was to be dominated by hyperbole.

But the *Daily Telegraph* did not confine itself to questions; it had some peripheral answers. The well-attested indoor target practice, for example (a recreation which, it will be remembered, would later appeal to Sherlock Holmes):

> We believe that we are correct in stating that these pistols, of which so much has been made, were little toy weapons with ivory handles—more popguns, in short, than pistols—picked up, in all probability, at some auction-room for nick-nacks, and with which Roberts's boy, as boys will do, had occasionally amused himself by loading them with powder and bullet, not much larger than would be required for a pea-shooter, and firing into the fireplace. He had missed his aim now and then, as was shown from a few dints on the marble jambs of the chimney.

Having confided to the public the results of his weekend cogitations on all the puzzling aspects of the case, the writer wound up with an insight that echoed the opinion, expressed less portentously, in other papers that morning:

> *There is a woman at the bottom of this horrible slaughter-house mystery.* There is a person who has gone by the name of Mrs. Murray, who must be sought out, and from whom evidence must be elicited. There are truths which must come to light, and which, until the patient in Charing-cross Hospital recovers entire consciousness, only this Mrs. Murray and the wife and son of Mr. Roberts can reveal. Ere the world is twenty-four hours older a lurid light will be thrown upon this ghastly secret; but we warn those not yet incriminated that the truth, the whole truth, and nothing but the truth must be told. In the end God will judge all things; but, pending the Eternal Fiat, it is the duty of man to use unrelaxing efforts in order that wickedness may be rooted out, and lies confuted, and the shedder of blood brought to justice.

Notwithstanding this prophecy, no lurid light was thrown upon the ghastly secret within the next twenty-four hours. But the prospect of its eventual shining guaranteed that the suddenly notorious address in Northumberland Street would not fade from the papers as the week proceeded.*

---

*From this point onward, the reader who wishes to follow either case continuously can do so by observing the section headings.

(Vidil)

The same editions of the Saturday papers that carried the first accounts of the frightful business in Northumberland Street contained the first detailed news of another murderous assault in a quite different setting. The Thursday edition of the *Morning Post* had had a single paragraph headed EXTRAORDINARY RUMOUR:

> A very painful story is current, which we trust is not well founded. A foreigner, well known in English society, is said to have attempted to murder his son, a young man nearly of age, who, upon attaining his twenty-first year, would be entitled to a large sum of money, which his father is supposed to have been unable to pay over to him. We withhold the name, in the hope that a speedy contradiction may be given to this almost impossible statement.

The next day's edition of the same paper, which Major Murray could have bought at London Bridge on his way to his encounter with William Roberts, ran a column and a half on the "painful story," naming names. The scoop—for that is what it seems to have been—was copied at length in the Saturday papers. EXTRAORDINARY ATTEMPT AT MURDER BY A FOREIGN NOBLEMAN, trumpeted the *Morning Chronicle* and the *Daily Telegraph*. THE CHARGE AGAINST BARON DE VIDIL, specified the *Times*. For the next fortnight, the two cases would together, on some days, command five or six columns of small type in the large folio pages that constituted the standard format of mid-Victorian daily papers. To every student of contemporary crime— and judging from the space the press allotted to the subject, they were legion—here was God's plenty.

The story that now unfolded was, they said,

> one of the most fearful incidents that has occurred in this country for many years past—an attempt not merely at murder, but the murder of a son by a father, a man of rank, of distinguished manners and position, moving in the best society. Nor is this crime one of darkness or of secrecy. It was perpetrated—if the accounts be true, and, unfortunately, there is no reason to doubt them—in broad daylight, within a few paces of a frequented high-road, in a populous neighborhood, and not many yards away from a palace which the perpetrator of the crime was apparently on his way to

"Baron De Vidil, French Adventurer in London Society" (From
Horace Wyndham: *Judicial Dramas* (London, 1927)

visit, after calling and being received as a welcome guest at another residence of the same royal family.

It was a mysterious melodrama that served as a perfect complement to the one starring Major Murray: a rural rather than an urban setting, though both were familiar to London readers and thus added to the shock value of both cases—murder in our very midst; an assault perpetrated in the open air rather than in a locked pair of dusty and cluttered rooms, and witnessed, or nearly so, by several people; the central figures a pair of men with the closest possible familial relationship rather than a pair who allegedly had never even met before, and one of them the bearer of an aristocratic title, not a retired army officer or, less impressive, a small-time bill discounter; the fortuitous involvement of a royal family, who surely had nothing in common with the occupants of Northumberland Chambers.

The *Morning Chronicle*'s account began in a style worthy of a popular circulating-library novelist:

> For some years past there has moved in London society an individual commonly known as the Baron de Vidil. In manners polished, in address insinuating; tall, graceful, elegant, and accomplished; of brown complexion, in ripened manhood, with hair still black and cut short, as of one who remembered his campaign in Algeria, and how very much that hair had been in the way when an Arab seized it in close contest; with whiskers just powdered by time; reputed wealthy; coming into society under the respectable name of the Orleans family, with the romantic reputation of fidelity to a fallen dynasty, no wonder that the Baron Alfred Louis Pons de Vidil readily found his way, under such auspices, into the heart and centre of London society. Such a man came, saw, and conquered.

As a necessary prerequisite to his conquest of London society, the baron (as he was not then called) had married, in 1835, Miss Susannah Jackson, co-heiress of a wealthy Hertfordshire gentleman. On the strength of this alliance, he became a member of the exclusive Travellers' Club and an ornament of the post-Regency fashionable set. (Major Murray's club, naturally, was the Army and Navy.) In due course, his wife bore him a son and then died. The son Alfred thrived, went to Cambridge, took his degree, and settled in rooms in Jermyn Street, St. James's (actually, around the corner at 40 Duke Street).

On Friday, 28 June, just a fortnight before Major Murray and "Mr. Gray" met in Hungerford Market, the father invited his son, twenty-three years of age, to breakfast with him at the Clarendon Hotel in Bond Street. Since the weather was fine, he proposed that they run down to Surrey to visit whatever members of the exiled French royal family happened to be at home. Accordingly, they took the 12:45 train from Waterloo to Twickenham, where they went to the inn near the station and picked up two horses that the baron had ordered sent down from London. They then set out for Claremont House, six or seven miles distant. This lovely house, the only complete surviving architectural work of "Capability" Brown, the celebrated landscape gardener, had earlier been owned by the Duke of Newcastle and Lord Clive of India. The prince regent, later George IV, had bought it for his only daughter, Princess Charlotte, who died in childbirth there. In 1848 the deposed king of France, Louis Philippe, had acquired it as the Orleanist palace-in-exile. He died two years later, and now his widow and several sons lived there.

Leaving their horses at a nearby inn, the two men walked to Claremont and, finding the queen not at home, spent an hour in affable conversation with one of her sons, the Duc d'Orléans (who would later fight in the American Civil War under General McClellan), and then returned to the inn, where they remounted their horses and rode slowly back toward Twickenham. It was at this point that the son, according to his later statement as summarized in the press, "became impressed with a strangeness in his father's manner, a singular absorption on his part, which led him, from some unknown impulse, to pay particular attention to his father's every action. He noticed that his father, who was a fine horseman, made his horse passage and curvet, and occasionally rear, but this had not the effect of making his son's horse even fidgety, for it was a dull beast." When they reached Hampton, the baron suggested that they stop off for refreshment, but his son, still feeling an undefinable apprehension and anxious to get rid of his horse, rode on. His father caught up with him and now proposed that they dine at Hampton. Again Alfred refused.

When they received their horses at Twickenham, the baron had neglected to take a whip and instead borrowed his son's, a lady's light riding model. Now, as they passed the gates of Bushey Park, the baron gave Alfred's horse a "sly cut," but the horse took no notice, and he returned the whip to his son. Reaching a fork in the road, the horsemen paused and the baron—oddly, because he knew the neighborhood well—asked his son which way was best. The latter urged that they go back the way they had come, by the high road to Twickenham. But the baron, without replying, turned his horse and chose the other route, a lonely lane going off to the left. The son, still feeling "a peculiar dread," asked him why he was taking this route. The baron murmured something about feeling ill and asked him to hold his horse while he dismounted. When the son asked whether he should ride on and fetch some brandy, the baron hastily declined and said that he would go and pay a visit to the Duc d'Aumale, another son of Louis Philippe, whose house was nearby. Through a series of errors they eventually found themselves at the stables behind Orleans House. Instead of going round to the front entrance, as Alfred supposed he would do, the older man, still leading his horse, conducted them away from the house, along a winding lane, with a high wall on one side and a tall, thick hedge on the other, until they reached a bend where he halted and looked both ways. No one was to be seen.

According to this first published account (later ones altered to a small degree the exact sequence of events), Alfred had ridden on a few paces and had his back to his father. He now felt a violent blow, and on looking round saw his father advancing on him, hand uplifted and holding some kind of weapon. Precisely what it was, where he had obtained it, and where he had meanwhile secreted it were to be crucial questions, never satisfactorily answered, in the trial to come. "The blow," said one paper, "fell a second time on the alarmed youth; and the father was about to complete his diabolical purpose by another and a finishing blow. The youth's hat had fallen off. There was nothing to save him. The murderer's blood was up. The poor boy's forehead, cut and battered, was streaming with gore. Impulse made him press on his horse, and as the horse rose to the spur it caught the blow on its head. That moment saved the youth's life, for he saw coming round the corner a man and a woman. Without an instant's delay, he slipped or fell from his horse, rushed towards the woman, and in an agony of terror, poor youth! clung to her knees, saying, 'Oh, protect me—save me.'"

The man was a young farm worker named John Rivers, who had been close enough to the spot to see the elder man strike the younger and to hear the youth cry out, "Oh! don't; pray don't!" and to see his father pursue him, after he had slipped from his horse, calling out, "Hoy, boy! Here is your hat!"

Now another person appeared, a bargeman named John Evans,

who said that he "saw the young Alfred's face covered with blood, and that he came crouching like some hunted and terrified beast all shuddering for its life, cowering down as he cried out, 'Help me; protect me; save me!'"

Meanwhile, both horses ran free. The baron, with what appeared to be a whip in his hand, ran up and cried, "What is it? What has happened?" and rushed toward a fence. The bargeman said there was nothing on the other side but a field leading to the Thames, but the baron climbed over it, in the process tearing his hands on the hook nails (tenter hooks) atop the fence, and disappeared behind some shrubs, about twenty or thirty yards away.

"The young de Vidil was bleeding profusely, and John Evans supporting him. 'Oh, I am so glad you are here,' said the poor young man, 'Do not, do not, leave me.' 'No, I'll not leave you,' replied John Evans; 'but how did it happen?' The youth opened his mouth to speak, but his eyes fixed with a terrified stare as he saw his father's eye steadily gazing on him, and he heard him murmur something about a wall and a fall. And so they proceeded, Evans supporting him bleeding to the nearest public-house on the road. 'Why did you get over the gate?' inquired John Evans of the Baron. 'To fetch assistance,' was the ready reply. 'How did it happen?' inquired John Everett, another labourer, who came up as he saw the group and the bleeding man. 'How did it happen?' 'Oh, the young gentleman stood up in his saddle to look over the wall,' was the father's reply, 'and his horse reared and so he fell;' but to John Evans he said the horse shied and threw the boy against the wall."

At the Swan Inn at Twickenham, where the riderless horses had already appeared and been secured, blood on the mane of one and on the saddle of the other, the young man's wounds were washed and a surgeon, Mr. Alfred Clark, summoned. Young Alfred de Vidil begged him to let his assistant accompany him back to London. The surgeon, "who imagined that something was not as it should be"—he was sure that no fall from a horse, but a blunt, heavy weapon, had caused those head wounds—consented. The three then returned to Alfred's rooms in Duke Street, where the baron insisted on staying with his terrified son until midnight. Nothing he could say or do succeeded in budging the surgeon's assistant from the bedside.

Early the next morning Alfred, his head heavily bandaged, fled to the home of his uncle William Parker, a county magistrate, at Ware, Hertfordshire. His father pursued him even there, in the form of a letter to Parker telling him that Alfred had seriously injured himself falling off his horse. (A minor question, never raised, was how he could have written a letter when his hands were injured by the tenter hooks on the fence he had clumsily climbed over.) Alfred, of course, told his uncle a different story, which he proceeded to embody in a formal deposition, and it was the substance of this story that appeared in the press on 13 July, side by side with the earliest narrative of the Northumberland Street drama. The newspapers added that the week after his alleged assault on his son the baron had dined at the Travellers' Club with several officials from the Foreign Office, and then, on the following Monday (8 July), he had fled to France. A warrant for his arrest was granted two days later, on the basis of his son's deposition and at the behest of the uncle, and a party of detectives set off for Paris. As early as Tuesday the *Times* (and doubtless other papers) possessed all the facts that had as yet become known. But, as the *Times* put it, "it was positively necessary for the ends of justice that as little publicity as possible should be given to the details," and the story was suppressed. When news arrived on Friday, 12 July, that the baron, "a member of the Jockey Club," as all the papers emphasized, had been arrested in Paris, there was no longer any reason to withhold it.

Whereas the speculation and gossip attending the Northumberland Street affair had begun only when the first news of it appeared in the Saturday papers, in the Vidil case they had had ten days' head start, beginning at the moment when young Alfred had sworn his accusation of his father. The inventive and swift-running rumor mills in the London clubs had immediately come into operation, and now the newspapers contributed to the output, especially by way of dispatches from their Paris correspondents. The *Morning Chronicle*'s man in Paris identified Alfred as the baron's son-in-law (in Victorian usage, the synonym of "stepson") and said that the young man had been left "a large fortune, with the condition that, in the event of his death," it should go to his mother's "second husband," the baron. "According to some accounts," added this correspondent, "it was in Scotland that the Baron attempted to commit the crime."

Other papers printed similarly erroneous dispatches from their Paris correspondents. The first that the *Daily News* received and printed (13 July) said that "a member of the Jockey Club was arrested this morning [Thursday] on a charge of having committed a murderous assault upon his wife's son by a former marriage, with the object of securing his fortune. The young man, only 20, was found, it is said, in the environs of Paris mortally wounded, but with sufficient strength left to denounce his murderer." The second dispatch from Paris, printed the following Monday, was longer, and even more richly wrong:

> Baron Vidil, as guardian to his step-son, would be liable to account for and pay over the fortune of the latter on his coming of age, and it was to escape this liability that he drew the young man to a lone place in the country, fell upon him, wounded him grievously, and left him for dead on the spot. So far all the accounts I have heard to-day agree. The monstrous deed was perpetrated in England several days ago. The story is that M. Vidil was seen galloping about near Twickenham, inquiring with much apparent distress of mind for his son, who had been making an excursion with him, and whom he had lost; that the peasants found in the fields a young man, wounded in several places, speechless. The step-father, it is said, sent for medical assistance, and sat by his victim's bed-side for two or three days, when he left, saying that urgent business required his presence in Paris; and it was after his departure that the youth sufficiently recovered to state the astounding fact that his legal and natural guardian and protector was his would-be murderer.

It says something for the intensity of interest the Vidil case stirred that the London papers would—gratuitously, one might think—print lavishly garbled capsule versions of the crime from abroad alongside what were, at the moment, relatively "authoritative" accounts put together in their London offices only a few miles from the scene.

The first "fact" mentioned in the *Daily News*'s Paris dispatch, that the baron had attempted to kill his son to escape paying him the inheritance to which he was entitled, was accepted at face value in the first editorial comments to be printed. The *Morning Chronicle*, for example, said that "he had injured the young man beyond redemption; he had squandered the fortune entrusted to his keeping, and the day of repayment was at hand." The only way he could devise to hide his malpractices was to murder the young man he had robbed.

At this early stage, Vidil's avarice was universally assumed to be the motive behind the crime; whether it had to do with money already misspent or money to be spent in the future, given the son's opportune demise, was a secondary issue. There was, therefore, little scope for speculation on that score. The best that newspapers could do, pending further developments, was to debate whether the baron was insane or merely extraordinarily villainous. The *Daily Telegraph*, however, recognized no such subtleties. The baron, it concluded, "can hardly hope to escape heavy punishment for one of the most detestable outrages ever recorded in the calendar of crime"—a fairly harsh judgment on a suspect who had not yet even been brought before a court of law.

MONDAY, 15 JULY– SATURDAY, 20 JULY (Murray)

The crowds lingered outside 16 Northumberland Street over the weekend, frustrated because (as was not always the case in Victorian times) the police, denying the freeborn Englishman's right to know and see all, had locked up the scene of the crime, "by what legal right it would be difficult to say," remarked one tart editorialist. There had been no significant developments in the case. The hospital had issued bulletins on the condition of Murray and Roberts, both of whom were under police guard: Murray improving, Roberts critical. The one incident that might have cast a glimmer of light on the dark proceedings ended in fiasco. On Saturday afternoon, Corrie, the Bow Street magistrate, had been notified that Roberts might talk. He and his chief clerk hurried to his bedside, where the following dialogue was reported to have occurred:

CORRIE: "I am the magistrate. I understand you want to speak to me."

ROBERTS (unable to speak above a whisper): "No; I only said I wanted some tea."*

The tea was provided and, said one news story, "he drank it greedily," though it is hard to understand how, in his condition, he managed to do so.

CORRIE: "Now I am ready to hear what you have to say."

ROBERTS (very indistinctly): "I can't speak; my face is too bad."

---

*The misunderstanding over rhyming words bore traces of the familiar patter of street puppet shows: in one version of the "last dying speech" in the Punch and Judy execution scene, the Hangman said, "You have been a very bad and wicked man," and the doomed Punch replied, "I want a slice of bread and jam."

CORRIE: "Do you feel able to say anything about this transaction?"

ROBERTS: "I am not able to talk about it."

CORRIE: "Would you like to tell me how it took place?"

ROBERTS: "I can't talk about it."

CORRIE (to those gathered around the bed): "It is useless for me
to remain. If there is any possibility of his making a statement, I can be
sent for."

On Monday, Murray's brother and his lawyer, Mr. Humphreys,
Jr., told the Bow Street magistrate that the major was eager to make a
full, formal statement as soon as the medical gentleman in attendance
allowed. Roberts, rallying somewhat—though he understandably
complained of a headache—volunteered a statement of his own, in
which he averred that he had never seen Murray before the encounter
in Hungerford Market; that the business that took them to Roberts's
chambers did, indeed, have to do with a loan to the Grosvenor Hotel
Company which a client of his named Sir R. Anstruther* proposed to
make; and that "on his arrival there the major first shot himself in the
back of the neck, and then attacked him [Roberts] with the tongs." He
refused to elaborate on these proceedings. Even had he been inclined
to do so, as the hours passed he became less and less capable of
speech.

He was only able to articulate a very few words [said the all-
knowing *Daily Telegraph*] and, as an instance of the painful difficulty with which he uttered any intelligible sound, we may mention that, in asking for water, he repeated the word "pump" in so
imperfect a manner as to be misunderstood for some space of
time. The intellectual choice of a word less difficult than the one
which he would ordinarily have used shows, also that the sufferer
was in full possession of his mental faculties. . . . Beside the
physical obstacles to Roberts's making any statement, it would appear that he had a strong repugnance to doing so. The surgeon,
wishing to see his tongue, inserted a finger at the side of his
mouth, and succeeded in partially opening it. At the moment,
however, when this was effected, the unfortunate man caught

---

*Sir Ralph Abercrombie Anstruther, fourth baronet (1804–63), was the son of
General Robert Anstruther, who had served with the Duke of Wellington in the Penin-
sular Wars. Two weeks later (30 July) the *Times* printed a brief note from him disclaim-
ing any connection with the case.

sight of the police constable, and, with an effort which must have cost him intense pain, from the fracture of his cheek-bone, screwed his lips tightly together. The presumption on the part of those who had watched him from the hour of his admission to the hospital was that, in this little action, he betrayed a nervous dread literally of opening his mouth.

On Tuesday Roberts lapsed into a coma. His condition improved the next day, but inflammation of the brain set in, and as a last resort the surgeon who had treated him on his arrival at the hospital operated to remove three or four large fragments of bone from his right temple. But Roberts died at 6:20 Thursday afternoon, just in time for Friday's *Daily Telegraph* to mix Grand Guignol horror with pathos in its vision of his last hours: "a mutilated creature, whose head was a mass of blood-stained pulp, one of whose eyes was a mere lump of purulent jelly, who, livid and gasping in what seemed the death agony, lay yesterday before us in the hospital ward, with his weeping wife by his side and a police officer at the bed's foot, . . . ere these lines were committed to print, . . . rendered up his soul to the Almighty."

Meanwhile, it was reported that earlier optimistic bulletins on Murray's condition were premature. Although the bullet that had embedded itself in a vertebra had been successfully removed, its passage had created a deep and dangerous wound in the throat, to minister to which the surgeon was "obliged to perform a very formidable operation." The major remained on the serious list. (A certain doubt may be attached to this particular report. If the major had been as garrulous as the papers made him out to be as they relayed his successive accounts of his adventure, the throat wound must not have been all that serious.)

On Saturday, 20 July, representatives of Roberts, deceased—his uncle, who was a solicitor in Spring Gardens, and the barrister he had briefed, William Campbell Sleigh*—appeared at Bow Street court. During the week, the newspapers had reported that the police, having taken possession of the rooms in Northumberland Street, had been examining the mass of disordered papers they found there. Hints

---

*Sleigh (1818–87) was a well-known barrister on the home circuit and in London criminal courts. An effective cross-examiner, he appeared in many cases at the Old Bailey and accepted the first brief for the Tichborne Claimant in that pair of long-running trials (1871–74). He went to Australia, whence the claimant had come, in 1877.

were dropped that they had found documents that shed some light on the mystery. Now the lawyers requested permission to conduct a search of their own. Corrie, however, told them that he was powerless to instruct the police in the matter; but Superintendent Durkin subsequently assured them that he would afford them every facility.

This was the state of affairs as the week drew to a close. The newspapers complained that their reporters were "but little in the confidence of the police or the connections of the friends of the combatants." Left to do their own detection, they raised numerous questions and implied a few answers—making bricks without straw as long experience in dealing with murky crimes had taught them to do. And in the absence of new, hard facts there were always rumors to fall back on. Major Murray was said to be one of three brothers, one of whom went to Australia, where he died. His widow, coming to England, placed her affairs in Roberts's hands. The major contested her claim to her late husband's estate. Said Saturday's *Morning Chronicle*:

> The police, from what we learn, believe that Major Murray saw Mr. Roberts meet a certain lady in Hungerford-market, and followed the two to the chambers of the latter. Was this the aforesaid widow? and why did the Major dog them to the rooms which it is presumed he entered? The Major says he ultimately found the door locked. Where is the key? Is it not possible that a third person locked the door on the outside? Mrs. Roberts asked after Mrs. Murray. What Mrs. Murray is this? Is she the Major's wife, or sister-in-law, or neither? Who and where is she? All this may be capable of "satisfactory explanation;" but anything more unsatisfactory than the case as it stands, can scarcely be conceived.

The *Daily Telegraph* on that same newsless day launched a variant of the same story, one significant difference being that in its version "Mrs. Murray" was not the major's sister-in-law:

> It is said . . . that Mr. Roberts and Mr., or Major, Murray, were passengers by the same boat to Hungerford Bridge; that they landed together, and walked through the market and the court which leads into Northumberland-street; that Major Murray, being in the rear, saw a lady, who has been permitted to enjoy the use of his name, greet Mr. Roberts familiarly and accompany him to the chambers opposite; finally, that Major Murray, having watched the pair within doors, gained an entrance and proceeded

to the back room on the first floor. The rest seems plain. The pseudo Mrs. Murray departed in haste, and an encounter soon followed, by whom begun it will be very hard to prove.

Clearly, the police had a great deal on their plate. But the press knew exactly where the solution lay. They need only heed the stentorian voice of the *Daily Telegraph* as it huffed and puffed: "Let the woman, of whom distorted tales are abroad, stand forth, and say what is and what is not true in all these rumours. Baseless or insubstantial they certainly are not. We know enough to assert this, have known it almost from the first, and warn those who have the official conduct of the case that time lost in bringing it to an issue can never be retrieved."

(Vidil)

To report that Vidil was arrested at the Jockey Club, "which was hemmed in by a cordon of police agents to prevent his escape," made a better story (in the *Daily News*), but the unremarkable fact seems to have been that Inspector Thornton of Scotland Yard and a colleague from the Sûreté apprehended him without incident at his home in the rue Saint Lazare and lodged him in the Prison Mazas. Initially there was some speculation whether he could be extradited, French and British law differing on the point. But the French authorities, perhaps after quiet consultation with the Foreign Office, raised no objection to his being returned to England, and he was brought back over the weekend.

He arrived at the Bow Street magistrate's court on Monday afternoon. News of his return having got out, the court and adjacent streets were densely crowded, some onlookers probably having come the short distance from that other focus of metropolitan interest, the locked premises in Northumberland Street. The baron was described in the press as "a spare, gentlemanly-looking man, about fifty years old," of medium height and wearing a large, flowing beard and mustache. He was dressed in a frock coat and light trousers. One reporter said he "looked nervous and anxious."

When the hearing got under way, the prisoner was formally identified by his brother-in-law, Alfred's Hertfordshire uncle, who testified that he had known him for some years. The baron's counsel, William Sleigh, who, as we have seen, was also briefed by William Roberts's uncle, now requested a remand, which was granted by the presiding

Examination of Baron De Vidil at Bow Street

magistrate, Mr. Corrie, another early participant in the Northumberland Street proceedings. Both would be busy men in the days to come.

At twenty minutes to six the baron was removed from the dock, where he had held his hand up to his face to conceal his agitation. As he was escorted from the building, he evidently did not see his son, "a delicate-looking man," who had been waiting in an anteroom, reluctant, said one paper, to proceed further in the matter. His father was taken in a police van to the House of Detention, "amidst the hootings and groans of the large crowd outside the court." It is impossible to determine, at this distance in time, how far their views coincided with those of the editorialists. Here, said that day's *Morning Chronicle*,

> we have a gentleman of rank and station, well received in English drawing-rooms, the guest of Royalty—for Royalty it still is, though fallen—a man against whom no word of reproach appears to have been ever raised, and who was a welcome visitor in the mansions of the aristocracy of France and England. This man—whose outward demeanour was so decorous, whose manners were as faultless as his dress, whose conscience, apparently, as stainless as his kid gloves—we suddenly discover meditating a crime above all others base and treacherous. His intended victim was not a sharper who had fleeced him at the gaming-table, a Lothario who had outraged his honour, or inflicted upon him one of those deep insults which it is supposed nothing but blood can wipe out. He was none of these, but, on the contrary, one whom he was bound to protect—his ward and step-son. But unhappily, as it would appear from the current reports, he had injured this young man beyond redemption; he had squandered the fortune entrusted to his keeping, and the day of repayment was at hand. Having thus inflicted a grievous injury upon his ward, the only means which the Baron de Vidil—for it is idle to keep back his name—could devise for hiding his malpractices, was to murder the young man he had robbed. This is, indeed, a stale and commonplace contrivance, and would not raise this little domestic tragedy above the ordinary level of vulgar crime, were it not for the elaborate means that were adopted for perpetrating it. . . . At present we have only common rumour to guide us; but, assuming the main outline to be true, and not a well-contrived hoax, we may thank the more prosaic imagination of our island, which has not witnessed a murder so deliberately planned since the day when Thurtell lured Weare to his destruc-

tion [1823] or the Mannings beguiled the luckless Connor to their back kitchen at Bermondsey [1849].

Preliminary judgment in the case was made more troublesome because, though the baron may well have been in legitimate possession of his title, for whatever it was worth, he was evidently not to the manner born. With Murray and Roberts there was no such doubt to cloud the issue: one was a retired army officer and the other a bill discounter, and that was that. The editorial writers knew where they stood. But the Frenchman? Gossip was circulating at this time in clubland and in newspaper offices which seems to have first appeared in print in the *Morning Chronicle* for 22 July:

> He has been represented as the most fascinating and accomplished of men. A member of the select and exclusive Jockey Club of Paris, and a foreign and honorary member of our own fashionable Travellers' Club here, he was at first represented as one of the *élite* of society—the observed of all observers—the pink of fashion and the mould of form—"a gentlemanly-looking man of fifty-five," who did not merely drive a gig* and graduate in respectability in such a middle-class way, but was an honored guest in the saloons of exiled princes, and having easy access to the tables of the noblest of our countrymen, he appeared to live upon a social eminence which might have provoked jealousy, but which freed him from any suspicion of heinous criminality. On the other hand he has been represented, with perhaps equal exaggeration, to have been certainly a *parvenu*, and perhaps a bore. He is said to have been the son of a glove-maker, and to have had, in his own person, some mysterious commercial connection with button-making, and to have either acquired his title by the purchase of a small Italian estate which conferred that empty distinction upon him, or else to have been the last plebeian metamorphosed into an aristocrat by the will and pleasure of the late Louis Philippe. It is doubtless, as a matter of gossip, interesting to that curious individual, the general reader—but it is a matter of perfect indifference in an English court of law whether

---

*A reference to a bit of testimony in the trial of John Thurtell and his accomplices for the murder of William Weare. Weare, the *Morning Chronicle* reported a witness as saying, "always maintained an appearance of respectability and kept a gig." Thanks to Thomas Carlyle's sardonic reference to "gigmanship," ownership of one of these modest conveyances had become an almost proverbial mark of respectability.

the accused is the undoubted scion of a family dating from the Deluge, or the most pushing, irrepressible, and objectionable of that terrible section of society, who are described as "distinguished foreigners."

A week later (29 July) the *Illustrated News of the World* supplied what it said were the true facts of the baron's career, replacing the *Morning Chronicle*'s hazy suggestions with specifics. In its unabashed prejudice, its rhetorical craftiness (prefacing the recital of the "facts" with a contrasting reference to "myth"), and its lightheartedness that permitted a waggish play on words (glovemaker/gauntlet), the paper's treatment of this vexed subject was faithful to the spirit of the press coverage at large:

Some people maintain that the tale of Baron Vidil attempting to murder his son is a myth; that there is no such person in existence, and that the whole thing was invented by the penny-a-liners. Such, however, does not appear to be the case. The baron is proved to be a really existing man, but, happily for the credit of the aristocracy, not of pure breed. The baron is the son of a glovemaker, who had shops at Grenoble and in Old Jewry, London. The glover advanced a considerable sum of money to Mr. de Mornay (*not Morny*),* a gentleman of high influence in the good old days of Louis Philippe. The glover could not recover his money, but he was ambitious—he would like to see his son a diplomatist. In those days the job was easily managed. Young Vidil, instead of being placed behind his father's counter, was sent off as attaché to the French Embassy at Stockholm, whence he was ultimately transferred to London. But as the glover became boisterous in his demands for his loan, with interest, young Vidil was converted into a baron, and the crimson ribbon of the Legion of Honour fluttered from his button-hole. The emancipated glover threw down the gauntlet to society, and under these colours he fought his way into English clubs and drawing-rooms, and ultimately married Miss Jackson. In consenting to this union, Mr. Jackson

---

*Charles Auguste Louis Joseph Morny (later Duc de Morny) was a Bonapartist politician with close ties to his half-brother, Napoleon III, whose coup d'état he had supported in 1851. He had been most recently in the news in November 1860, when he successfully urged the adoption of several cosmetic "liberalizing" measures designed to stem the rising democratic and clerical opposition to the repressive régime. I have not identified the Mr. de Mornay who was not to be confused with him.

insisted on his daughter's fortune being settled upon her issue. Some barons fancy they may do as they like in England. This is rather a mistake.

In a filler paragraph printed after Vidil's trial, the *Times* added to the dossier a few details that either amplified or differed from the *Illustrated News of the World*'s capsule biography. Prior to the Revolution of 1830, it said, Alfred's father, Alphonse Vidil, "carried on the business of a glove manufacturer in the rue Richelieu, Paris, while his son fulfilled the duties of a *commis voyageur* to the establishment. In this capacity the latter made frequent visits to England, and became known to the principals of several commercial houses in London." The young man's patron was Marshal Soult, a hero of the Napoleonic Wars who was twice minister for war under Louis Philippe. Through his influence Vidil was appointed attaché to the French embassy at Vienna (not Stockholm), and when the marshal attended Queen Victoria's coronation in 1837 as ambassador extraordinary, Vidil was in his entourage. According to the *Times*, Vidil had already been ennobled. (Counting the two alternatives in the *Morning Chronicle*'s account, this was the fourth version of how and when he acquired the title of baron.) It was from this time onward that he was "a recognized member of the distinguished circles of both capitals," Paris and London. The *Times* said nothing about the loan owed to the ambitious glove-maker—an element in the story that would prove to be the only feature the Vidil and Murray cases had in common.

Commercial traveler for a Parisian (or was it a provincial?) glove-maker—diplomat—possessor of a foreign title—member of the Jockey Club and the Travellers' Club—widowed husband of an heiress—intimate of royalty—and a would-be murderer too? This was the spice that distinguished the Vidil mystery from the one in Northumberland Street.

On Tuesday an unforeseen difficulty arose. Inspector Thornton reported to Corrie that one of the key witnesses in the case, the farm worker John Rivers, had had a serious hemorrhage—he was consumptive—and was not expected to live. Because he was the only actual eyewitness to Vidil's attack on his son, his testimony, delivered in the presence of the accused, was crucial to any criminal action that might be undertaken. Unless he identified the baron as the assailant and young Vidil as the victim, the case would have to be dropped for lack of evidence, the son's "information" (complaint) notwithstanding.

The Northumberland Street case being in abeyance for the moment—this was the day that Roberts sank into a coma—Corrie said he would be free to travel down to Twickenham and receive the deposition. Inspector Thornton said that this would not be necessary, because a local magistrate would serve as well. While the party was being assembled, the baron's solicitor, Mr. Wontner, asked to see the son's complaint. The official document substantially corresponded with the version that had appeared in the press, though it brought out in greater detail, partly by quoting the several exchanges that had taken place between the two, the baron's indecisiveness as he led his son down one lane after another, searching, it seemed, for a suitably obscure spot in which to perpetrate his assault. When they paused at the fork of the road, the elder Vidil, his son said, "gave me to understand that he was suffering from bowel complaint. I said, 'Won't you turn back and go to the inn?' He said, 'Will you hold my horse?' I said, 'How shall I hold it?' meaning, was I to remain on my own horse or get down? He said, 'Oh, never mind.' . . . We walked back to the main road. In passing the inn I urged him to take some brandy there. He said, 'No, no, thank you—it does not look a very nice place.' When in the lane he told me of his stomach-ache, I said, 'If I had known that I would have dined at Hampton, as you asked me to.' He said, 'That is very kind.'" These courteous words seemed not to comport with the picture that otherwise emerged, of a villain, madman or not, on the verge of assaulting his son.

Inspector Thornton and Baron de Vidil went down to Twickenham, there to meet the several lawyers concerned with the case, the son, and his uncle, Mr. Parker. (The press did not report how, if at all, father and son greeted each other.) A crowd gathered in the village to stare at them. But now a fresh difficulty arose. Despite Thornton's assurance that a local magistrate could be found, a search failed to turn one up; one gentleman had gone out to dine, a second was attending his daughter's wedding, and a third had not yet returned home. More than an hour elapsed before a properly qualified Colonel Donnethorne arrived at the police station, shortly followed by a second magistrate, one Captain Murray. To identify him with the Captain Murray who had just finished arranging for legal counsel to represent his brother, the major, would be to demand too much of coincidence.

The legal formality now being in place, the party moved to the bedside of the critically ill witness.

Here [said the *Daily News*], in one of two little tenements called Zion Cottages, within a short distance of the lane in which the alleged attack was made, and near the river side, lay poor John

Rivers, a young labouring man, in the last stages of decline. His bedroom was small but very clean, and in the front upper room adjoining, his two little children, both under three years of age apparently, were lying upon a bed, the oldest restless and ill, the youngest for some time asleep, but presently waking up and compelling its afflicted mother to leave the bedside where she had been watching the effect of the examination upon the sick man with natural anxiety.*

The sick man's deposition, often interrupted by coughing spells, verified what had already been reported. He had been one hundred yards away from the horsemen when he saw the older of the two, who was dismounted, strike the other with what might have been a whip handle; at least it had a shiny knob. He had watched as the young one rode off, blood pouring down his face. Then he took the youth's hat to the Swan public house, where he found him being treated by a surgeon. The landlord of the Swan gave him a shilling.

Rivers was asked to point out the older man he spoke of from the dozen or so who crowded the room. He did so, and repeated the identification when the baron put on his white hat. When young Alfred was brought into the room, Rivers immediately identified him also. The deposition having been read back to him, he affixed his mark to the document and the delegation left.

On Wednesday, the *Times* printed a dispatch from its Paris correspondent, which appeared to be an effort on someone's part to put some distance between the accused and exiled French royalty.

I am positively assured [he wrote] that the statement of the Baron de Vidil having been on terms of much intimacy with the members of the Orleans family at Claremont is without foundation. The members of that family are, I believe, accessible to most persons of fair standing and character, French or otherwise; but this does not necessarily imply frequent and intimate intercourse. M. de Vidil, since his return to France after the death of his wife in England, lived a good deal in society, entertained much, and, as he was reputed rich, had, of course, a vast number of acquaintances who may have passed for friends, and who generally wish to pass for friends so long as one is prosperous. He certainly had

*In response to this affecting scene, the Bow Street magistrate subsequently received three contributions to aid the dying man's wife and family: a pound from one A. J. Ferries, five shillings from "J.W.L.," and two shillings in stamps from an anonymous donor.

among his "friends" several of the warmest and most devoted friends of the Orleans Government (while it lasted), such as the Mornys, the Walewskis, &c; but he was on equally good terms with Bonapartists, perhaps before, but undoubtedly since, the Bonapartists have been at the top of the wheel. He was, if I remember well, among the select guests at Fontainebleau last year during the sojourn of the Emperor.

At three o'clock that afternoon, the Bow Street court and the streets outside were again jammed with the curious and expectant as Vidil's examination was about to get under way. Corrie shared his bench with a distinguished guest list that included two peers, at least two members of Parliament, and several other gentlemen with influence in the right places. As soon as the baron took his seat in the dock, "he covered his face with his hands to avoid the gaze of the persons on the magistrate's bench," who may very well have included clubman acquaintances of his. He did not raise his eyes throughout the proceedings; even when a note was handed to him, he rested it on his knees to avoid the necessity of raising his head.

Appearing for the plaintiff was thirty-eight-year-old Charles Edward Pollock, member of a distinguished family of lawyers who was to take silk five years later and receive a knighthood in 1873. Immediately a difficulty arose that made yesterday's search for a magistrate in Twickenham seem a trifle in comparison. Called to the stand, Alfred de Vidil proved to be a "rather pale young gentleman," as one reporter described him, with "a large forehead, aquiline nose, high sunken cheeks, and a finely formed but not very expressive mouth." When he was asked to swear on the Bible, he sprang a surprise that instantly placed the case on a new, perplexing footing. A modern journalist would undoubtedly have called the moment a bombshell: Vidil, the complainant, refused to testify.

In a voice so low and trembling as to be almost inaudible, he said, "I am placed in most painful circumstances. I am not willing to proceed any further, and I hope I shall not be pressed to give evidence. I am not well, and I don't think—I don't know (a pause)—I don't think I can give evidence. I do not know what will become of my father if—if I am pressed. I had better state honestly to you that when I asked for the warrant I did so only for my own protection, not thinking it would lead to this. I did not think they would succeed—that it would be executed. I did not think they would find my father. I cannot tell what effect it will have upon me, but I hope I shall be able to undergo whatever you may put upon me or require if I refuse to give evidence. If you insist upon my speaking I am in a dreadful position. You do not know all. I understand that my father has accused me, to a certain extent—he has made a charge against me. If he says anything against me, then I shall be compelled to tell everything. I wish him to know that if he insists I must tell all."

Both Pollock and Sleigh hastily rose to address the magistrate, but because they spoke simultaneously and each interrupted the other, their voices canceled each other out .

"One more remark I wish to make before withdrawing from this matter," Vidil resumed. "Many gentlemen have kindly moved for me and assisted me. I wish to state that they have done so only at my request, and for the protection of my life. I do not wish to say anything against my father, unless he insists on—He has been a most unfortunate man, and I do not know if it is not the duty of children to bear even more than I have done—to bear anything for the sake of their parents. It is very painful. I cannot say more."

Sleigh got to his feet again. "If this young gentleman thinks that any insinuation is made against him, if he labours under that impression, I must say that it is not so, and I hope he will dismiss it from his mind."

POLLOCK: "This witness is called for me, and I object to your interference, subject to the magistrate's opinion. I have refrained from doing so for obvious reasons."

SLEIGH: "If he refuses to be sworn?"

CORRIE: "It scarcely amounts to that."

SLEIGH: "He has done so substantially."

CORRIE (to Vidil): "It is my duty, however I may sympathise—as we must all sympathise with you—it is my duty to tell you that you must be sworn."

SLEIGH: "If the young gentleman feels in his own breast a disinclination—"

POLLOCK: "I object."

SLEIGH: "This is an exceptional case. If he objects, surely in such a case he ought not to be subjected to any pressure."

CORRIE: "I have already said how painful a duty it is; still, I must swear you to tell the truth and the whole truth."

VIDIL: "I have been injured as much as any man, and have good reasons to state the truth even without an oath; but it is the duty of children to abstain from proceedings, and I look rather—"

CORRIE: "If you will not give evidence I must send you to prison. Do you refuse to give evidence?"

VIDIL: "I do."

CORRIE: "Then you will be sent to prison from time to time. I must send you to the House of Correction for seven days unless you give evidence."

The young man was removed in custody of the jailer, and counsel and magistrate went to confer in an adjoining room. After twenty minutes they returned, and Sleigh asked for an adjournment until Friday. This was granted. He then made another request, that the baron, "who has suffered severely since he has been in prison on this charge [i.e., three days], may be admitted to bail, not in any trifling amount, but in such large and substantial terms as you, sir [Corrie], may think the importance of the case requires." This request was not granted. Then Pollock made an application of his own, that young Vidil be placed in the custody of his relatives and friends. Corrie did not like the idea: "I cannot suffer such a refusal as he has been guilty of, in open court, to pass over without protest," and in any event, he would be in jail only little more than a day. But Pollock persisted: "I must say, from what I have learned, that many of the young gentleman's friends are fearful, from the present state of his health, of the result of any imprisonment being inflicted on him." Uncle Parker spoke up: "I am afraid, your worship, that his health will break down completely if he is taken away from his friends and confined in a prison." Corrie, however, thought that "the confinement may bring him to a sense of his duty." The young man's doctor was called forward "and expressed his opinion that in the peculiar temperament of the son at the present moment it might seriously injure him to detain him in prison." Corrie persisted: "Would it be dangerous?" "I cannot say it would endanger his life, but it may incapacitate him for some time to appear here. I mean that his liberation is highly important to him."

Corrie then backed down. Ordering the son to be brought into the room, he said: "I am told that if I do not send you to prison for the present, but return you to your friends instead, you may more likely, after communication with them and the legal gentlemen here today, be brought to a proper sense of your duty. But I must tell you that you will be bound, sooner or later, to tell the whole truth. It is your duty to your Sovereign, and to society in general, to do so, and ultimately you must perform that duty."

"I am extremely obliged to you, sir," said Alfred, and the court adjourned. Father and son went their separate ways, one to Clerkenwell jail, the other to Hertfordshire. This time, to avoid the vocal attentions of the crowd outside, the baron was put in a cab rather than a police van, but despite this effort to avoid trouble, several skirmishes took place in front of the court, and one young man who assailed a policeman was "fined for his impudence."

On Friday the crowd caused even more trouble. At noon, three hours before the hearing was scheduled to resume, it was impossible for persons having other business in the court, mostly answering summonses, to enter. A few minutes before three, a police van drew up and the crowd rushed to watch the baron descend. But "instead of anybody coming out," the press reported, "two miserable women were escorted into the vehicle, which then departed. Great disappointment was manifested as soon as the truth became known that the Baron de Vidil was already in court," the police having delivered him to the building at ten o'clock that morning.

Inside, every place was taken, and Corrie again had as guests on the magisterial bench a full complement of dignitaries: one paper named a dozen and then added "&c." The course of justice continued to wash against an immovable obstacle. Pollock had to tell the magistrate that no effort by himself or by Vidil's relatives could move the young man to reconsider his refusal to testify. He remained as mute as the late William Roberts had, although in the latter case obstinacy was reinforced by grievous physical disability. Since the case now lacked a plaintiff, Pollock felt obliged to withdraw from the prosecution, and for a moment it appeared as if the action against Baron de Vidil would have to be dropped. But Inspector Thornton then announced that Sir Richard Mayne, commissioner of the Metropolitan Police, had instructed him to pursue it as a police prosecution. This evidently was a strategy for keeping the case alive until the possibility of turning it into a government prosecution was explored.

This formality having been taken care of, Sleigh rose to repeat his request that the baron be freed from jail under surety to keep the peace toward his son. The room resounded with groans and hisses, and Corrie issued the customary rebuke and threat from the bench. "I am sorry to hear that expression of feeling," said Sleigh, "for I cannot help thinking that what has occurred between father and son had made a great impression on the minds of most people"—a reasonable inference from the space it occupied in the press and the crowds it drew to Bow Street.

Alfred de Vidil was called to the witness box. "He stood for some minutes," said one reporter, "regarding the magistrate with a fixed and determined gaze [unlike his father, who again sat in the dock with head lowered]—the resolute expression strangely contrasting with the frail body and sickly face." Corrie once again urged him to take the oath and give testimony, but once again he refused.

"I have received information on oath from the young man in the box," Corrie told the audience, referring to the complaint that had set the legal machinery in motion, "which, if it is repeated before me—"

Young Vidil interrupted: "Excuse me, sir, I wish to say that—" A long pause.

Corrie: "Do you wish to address me before I proceed with my observations?"

A silence of two or three minutes followed. Whatever it was that Vidil meant to say, he thought better of it. Corrie continued, asserting that to permit a key witness—indeed, the one who had sworn the warrant in the first place—to persist in his refusal and not suffer an appropriate penalty would set a most undesirable precedent. Moreover, he found himself in an untenable position: he could not serve simultaneously as public prosecutor and magistrate. He therefore proposed to seek the advice of the home secretary, Sir George Cornewall Lewis. He warned Vidil that if the government decided to take up the prosecution, "he will be compelled to perform that duty, or undergo the penalty which the law inflicts upon persons who act in a similar manner." Meanwhile, the young man could go home if he undertook to appear when the hearing was resumed on Monday. Vidil did so undertake, warning, however, that if he were sworn, he could not guarantee to tell the truth—a rare instance of perjury openly promised. Corrie assured him that all that was required of him at present was that he show up, and with this understanding, the session adjourned.

And so the first week of the baron's ordeal by law (and, as far as that is concerned, by press) ended in an impasse. The *Daily Telegraph*'s opinion, printed that morning, remained pertinent that night. "It would certainly appear very much like a failure and a perversion of equity, if not of justice," it said, "if this entirely innocent and blameless young man were to be subjected to a penal incarceration of indefinite duration, while his wicked and unnatural parent went scot free." Clearly, Alfred had not foreseen the complications his accusation would breed; all he had evidently desired was to have his father bound over to keep the peace. Instead, he had laid the baron open to a charge of attempted murder, a capital offense in English law, even though in practice it was not often punished by death. Now he had placed himself in a situation in which "the law is explicitly and inexorably against him."

He *must* be sworn, says Mr. Corrie—and that excellent magistrate has the law on his side—or he must go hebdomadally to gaol, *in saecula saeculorum.* The very stringency, however, of the law is calculated to defeat its successful operation. If Alfred de Vidil persists in refusing to give evidence, it will become morally, if not physically, impossible to carry out against him the penalties with which recalcitrant witnesses are menaced. Mr. Corrie may commit him once, twice, or thrice; but he cannot go on sending him to the House of Correction for ever. The humanity and the proper feeling of society would revolt at such an aggravation of torture inflicted upon a young man whose only fault was that he understood the fifth commandment too literally, and that he continued to honour and revere a parent long after that parent had forfeited all claims to his esteem or his affection.

It was a frustrating, not to say bleak, prospect for all concerned.

MONDAY, 22 JULY– THURSDAY, 25 JULY (Murray)

An autopsy was performed on Roberts's body on Friday, 19 July, and the coroner's inquest opened the following Monday in the board room of Charing Cross Hospital. Sleigh represented the widow and family; Mr. Humphreys, Jr., appeared in behalf of the major, whose brother, Captain Murray, was present throughout the proceedings. The number of witnesses called, including several policemen, and the detailed nature of the testimony elicited led to Sleigh's protest, the next day, that what was normally a routine inquiry into the cause of death had been turned into a "police case." The coroner, Mr. St. Clair Bedford, replied that the police were present at his express request: "If they were not assisting me we should be here for a month." (Sleigh: "I take it on myself to say, without instructions, that the gentleman who instructs me is too good-hearted to desire to hurt the feelings of either Mr. Durkin or Mr. M'Kenzie, or any of the force under their control." Humphreys: "As the remark did not come from our side, sir, I need make no observation.") The fact, however, was that, whatever its precise legal status, the inquest served in effect as a trial for murder, lacking only an indictment, and the verdict the coroner's jury would reach was equivalent to the one that would be reached by the jury in a court of law that was formally responsible for deciding the major's guilt or

Mr. Sleigh, Counsel for the Roberts Family, and Mr. Humphreys, Counsel for Major Murray

innocence. Never before had a "mere" inquest commanded the London headlines as this one did, although there would be a similar situation in the famous Bravo case (the "Balham mystery") in 1876.

After viewing Roberts's remains, the jury began to hear witnesses. Mr. Skegg and Mr. Canton, the surgeons who had cared for Roberts as well as Murray, gave professional testimony as to the extent and gravity of Roberts's injuries. Their post-mortem examination had revealed that these were so numerous and various that his death could be assigned to no one particular cause. One blood clot against the brain was as large as a pigeon's egg, another the size of a shilling. They concluded, not surprisingly, that the horrible visitation on Roberts's head had been delivered by "a weapon of some description," probably a blunt one. In view of the number of ad hoc weapons found in his room, all bearing signs of recent employment, the use of the singular would seem to have been an oversimplification.

Thomas Clay and William Clark, the workmen in the yard, recalled their respective roles in that frantic hour in Northumberland Street ten days earlier. A fresh witness, whom the press had some-

The Inquest on Roberts's Body at Charing-Cross Hospital

how overlooked, was a young dressmaker named Mary Lines, who lived on the ground floor of Number 15. She testified that while she was eating lunch in the sitting room at the back of the house she heard the noise of what she took to be falling planks, followed by "some high words" between men in the first-floor room next door. After certain intervals she heard the same noise, followed by that of crashing glass, and saw a man drop from the wall of Number 16. He then ran through her house to the street, leaving spots of blood in the passage.

Sergeant Golden described his actions as the first policeman on the scene. Then it was Henry Ransom's turn. He recounted the story Murray had told him on the way to the hospital and confirmed that he had not taken any notice of the gunshots in the room below his office because for the past year Roberts had been in the habit of firing off his pistols there. "For the last two months," he continued, "there had been constant firing in his room. One day I asked him what he was doing, when he said, 'Well, the pistols had been lying there for the last six or seven years, and I thought I would have a little practice with them.'" Ransom had seen the small pistols but never the large pair.

The jury was about to be taken to inspect the scene of the crime when Roberts's uncle, the solicitor, asked permission to go with them. The following sharp exchange ensued:

HUMPHREYS: "I must object to any one going to the house with the jury."

ROBERTS: "But surely Mr. Humphreys will not object to me."

HUMPHREYS: "Mr. Roberts is the very person to whom my objection points."

ROBERTS: "But I really have an object in going there."

HUMPHREYS: "But I must object."

ROBERTS: "I will undertake not to speak one word to the jury."

SUPERINTENDENT DURKIN: "I do not think, sir, there can be any objection to Mr. Roberts going to the premises. I suppose his object is to see that no one speaks to the jury."

ROBERTS: "That is my object, and I cannot be prevented, for the premises are ours."

HUMPHREYS: "They may be; but you will not get in."

CORONER: "Perhaps the best way is that I should go to the premises, for then the jury will be before me in court."

Ruffled feathers having been smoothed, the expedition took place as required.

When the inquest resumed the next morning, Constable Arber recounted his actions and observations after he met Ransom and

Murray in Craven Court and was dispatched by the latter to Northumberland Street. He added that Roberts's pockets proved to contain several visiting cards bearing his name and several more bearing that of John Francis Walker, solicitor, some tickets to the Crystal Palace, half a railway return ticket, and a small leather purse containing percussion caps. Like other witnesses, Arber testified that Roberts had stubbornly refused to give any information on the circumstances of his late encounter. When medicine was offered him at the hospital, he spat it out.

The next witness but one (Constable Langley's brief testimony intervening) was Inspector Mackenzie, who proved to have had slightly better luck with the reticent Roberts. When he first attempted to question him, on Friday, Roberts had said, "My head is too bad." But late the next night, an examination lasting a quarter of an hour elicited disjointed answers which Mackenzie rearranged for clarity's sake: "I sat down by his bed-side, and said, 'Do you know me; my name is M'Kenzie?' and he said, 'Oh yes, I know you, Mr. M'Kenzie.' I said, 'Will you tell me how this occurrence took place; how you came to receive all these injuries about the head?' He said, 'Yes, a man named Murray done it.' I said, 'Tell me how, Mr. Roberts.' He said, 'He got the tongs, attacked me, and hit me over the head with it, and struck me with a glass bottle.' He then said, 'I will tell you more particularly.' I said, 'Did you know Murray before?' He said, 'I had seen him before, but had not spoken to him before.' I said, 'Did you meet him by accident or by appointment?' He said, 'By accident in Hungerford Market, and he came to my offices with me about a loan.' He then said, 'Murray shot himself in the neck, and attacked me with the tongs like a demon, and struck me with a glass bottle.' I then asked him what was the amount of the loan he was to give, and he said '£50,000.' I asked if he would wish to make a deposition before a magistrate, and he said, 'No, I have nothing more to say.' I said, 'Do you think you will get better?' He said, 'Yes, I think I do.'"

Mackenzie told the coroner and jury that when he made a further search of the premises on the preceding Friday, a week after the event (he had initially searched them within hours after the affray), he discovered in a linen hamper in the front room three shirts and a handkerchief, and in the folds of the carpet a towel, all of them bloodstained. In an oak cabinet was a razor, also—he assumed—bloodstained, although later testimony suggested that the red stain was either currant jelly or some unidentified resinous substance. But the discovery that finally pointed the way to the truth was a bloodied blotter on the writing table in the rear room. It preserved bits of handwriting: "Mrs. Murray, Elm Lodge, Tottenham" . . . "I cannot rest" . . . "Send by bearer."

SLEIGH (on behalf of Roberts's family): "Have you ascertained the name of the person who lives at the address on this blotting paper—at Elm Lodge?"

MACKENZIE: "I have."

SLEIGH: "Is it a lady who lives there?"

MACKENZIE: "Yes; a lady who passes by the name of Mrs. Murray."

SLEIGH: "Did you ascertain her Christian name?"

MACKENZIE: "Yes; Anna Maria."

HUMPHREYS (representing Murray, and addressing the coroner): "I may mention, sir, that I propose to tender that lady as evidence."

This promising line of examination was then dropped, and for a time the questioning centered, as it had in the earlier part of Mackenzie's occupancy of the witness chair, on minutiae relating to the condition of the rooms and what it implied about the precise nature and order of the fatal sequence of events. Then, by one of those random intrusions that every so often relieve the plodding monotony, repetition, and seeming nitpicking we find in detailed reports of English criminal proceedings, a witness was heard whose brief testimony, though adding not a grain to the resolution of the mystery, offers the modern reader a sudden authentic glimpse of the trivial texture of everyday life in which such cases are embedded. A painter named Richard Timms said that on the morning of the incident he was cleaning the staircase and taking up the matting at 16 Northumberland Street. About twelve o'clock the occupant of the first floor, whom he knew as Mr. Roberts, "asked me to go an errand for him. He asked me if I would get a linnet, saying I would get one at the top of St. Martin's lane on the left-hand side. He said I might give about 9d. for it, and he gave me a shilling to do so. He did not say distinctly, but he inferred I might keep the change. He said, 'There's a shilling.' I went immediately for the linnet, and was away about half an hour, and when I came back the place was in the hands of the police. Finding the place in confusion, I placed the linnet on the top of the letter-box, close by the door, and there I left it. The linnet [later] was found there dead."

So there was an additional casualty at 16 Northumberland Street. Neither lawyer wished to examine Timms, although his being sent on an errand at that moment suggested that Roberts had a strong interest in his not being nearby when something unsettling was about to occur inside the office.* (It seems likely that it was for the purpose of getting Timms out of the way that Roberts left the room momentarily after he seated Major Murray at his writing table.) The next witness was Mrs. Eliza Tyler, head nurse at the Charing Cross Hospital, who seems to have regarded herself as an amateur sleuth who could obtain results where the professionals failed. Roberts, she said, "seemed more disposed to speak to me than to the police, and therefore I put a few questions to him. I did so the day after his admission. I said to him 'How did you come hurt in this manner? Who has done it? How did you get beaten in this manner?' He said, 'Murray has done it.' I replied, 'What did you do to him?' He said, 'Nothing.' I said, 'How did Major Murray become shot?' He replied, 'He shot himself.' I said, 'Did he shoot himself first and beat you afterwards?' He said, 'He did shoot himself first and beat me afterwards.' He said, 'He beat me with the tongs and bottle.' He was perfectly sensible; but he complained of pain in his head. I thought it was very strange that he should say that the major shot himself first and beat him afterwards. I asked him if he knew Major Murray. He said he had seen him before, but had never spoken to him before. He said he thought Major Murray belonged to the Hotel Company, which wanted money, and if Major Murray went to his office he could effect it. He did not say whether Major Murray had known him before or not."

Now Roberts's son, whom Henry Ransom in his testimony called "Willie," was heard. After deposing that both rooms were clean and in good order when he last saw them, a week or two before the combat, and that he himself had fired at the mantelpiece the preceding Wednesday, he was shown the blotting paper and identified the handwriting as his father's. Then the coroner took up the questioning:

"Do you know Major Murray?"

"Yes, by sight."

"Can you explain how you came to know him by sight?"

"My father and I were passing along the Strand in March last, when he said, 'There is Major Murray.'"

"Is that the only occasion on which you saw him?"

---

*Just why Roberts specified a bird rather than any other article ninepence might buy remains a mystery. Presumably he did not have in mind Wordsworth's early poem "The Reverie of Poor Susan," inspired, said the poet, by "the affecting music of [caged] birds hanging . . . in the London streets during the freshness and stillness of the Spring morning." Roberts had other things on his mind than the "note of enchantment" the bird—a thrush in that case—sang to Wordsworth.

Willie Roberts,
Son of the Deceased

"I saw him once more on the landing leading to my father's office as I was coming out of the door."

"At what time of the day?"

"About three or four o'clock."

"On what day?"

"About the middle of April."

"You say he was on the landing; was he going up or down?"

"He had come up, and was on the landing."

"Where were you going?"

"To the London and Westminster Bank, to cash a cheque."

"Whose cheque?"

"My father's."

"Was he at home at the time?"

"He was."

"Did you ever hear your father speak of Major Murray?"

"He has often said he has been out with Major Murray. In fact, the name of Major Murray has been mentioned by him more than that of any other person. He has often said, 'I've been out all day with the major. I've been at the Grosvenor Hotel.' He did not say anything about the business they transacted. This is two or three months past. I have never written the name of Murray, nor 'Major' Murray. I have seen two letters addressed by my father to Major Murray. I think that was in April."

"Do you know if any person made any communications between Major Murray and your father?"

"Do you mean a gentleman?"

"Yes; any gentleman?"

"No, sir."

"You've laid a stress on the word gentleman. Do you know any other person who has made a communication to your father?"

"I have seen letters from Mrs. Murray to my father."

"Have you seen the contents of them?

"No; he has told me. He generally told me where letters came from."

"Has your father, then, had transactions with Mrs. Murray?"

"She called there frequently."

Mr. Sleigh then took over the questioning, in response to which Roberts reiterated and added particulars to what he had already said: the Murray in the hospital was indeed the Murray his father had pointed out to him, saying he had often been "out with him," and the one he saw on the landing. "I first heard of Major Murray's name at the commencement of this year and thence continuously. I recollect the address on one of the letters to Major Murray was somewhere in Pimlico. I have posted letters in my father's handwriting to a Mrs. Murray; about four, extending over a period of three or four months. I have seen the pistols in my father's chambers two years; but he has told me he has had them eight years. My father was not a quarrelsome, irascible man; he was of a quiet disposition. I have seen the lady I call Mrs. Murray calling at my father's chambers since about last October. Her visits were once or twice a week, generally in the afternoon. I used to leave at four o'clock, and my father used generally to come home about ten. The lady's visits were sometimes at one, two, or three o'clock. If I've left at four I have left her there. I have left her with my father in his chambers. I last left her there about a fortnight or three weeks before this occurrence."

Then it was Humphreys's turn to examine the witness. As young Roberts sorted out the persons and firms listed outside 16 North-umberland Street, it became apparent that they formed a loose partnership whose main business was the issuance, discounting, and collection of "bills of acceptance" or promissory notes—a low-grade occupation, notorious in Victorian fiction, that was the nemesis of imprudent men (and, as we shall soon see, an occasional woman) who spent more than they had and were consequently in urgent need of a loan. That the several associates shared a common mailbox, the scene of the unfortunate linnet's demise, enhanced the impression that together they offered a complete loan service under one roof, from the first necessitous application to the final issuance of a writ against the delinquent debtor.

There was no Nicholson in Nicholson and Company; perhaps at the suggestion of Roberts, whose wife's maiden name it was, it had been assumed by a Mr. Stocqueler, whose association with Roberts, whatever form it took, had ended some nine months previously.* Stocqueler had acted as an "army agent," dealing in commissions, which at that date continued to be bought and sold like commodities or chattels. John Francis Walker was a solicitor, whose letters the elder Roberts wrote and signed in his absence and whose summonses the younger Roberts was employed to deliver. Completing the web was the London and West End Mercantile Agency, composed solely of an accountant who shared Walker's office and also had one in King William Street in the City. His name was John Singleton Copley Hill, the first three names being those of the celebrated Boston-born artist who spent most of his career in England, and of the artist's namesake

---

*If men are known by the company they keep, the recent presence of Stocqueler among them was an oblique indication of his associates' character. Joachim Heyward Stocqueler (or Siddons: no one seems to be sure which was his real name) was one of those shabby and shadowy, if not actually shady, persons whom one repeatedly encounters by accident in the now obscure byways and alleys of Victorian London. A man of many occupations, none of them lastingly lucrative, he had spent many years in India as a journalist and compiler of guidebooks. After returning to London in 1843, he wrote or edited several military memoirs and handbooks for soldiers, composed burlesques and extravaganzas for the Lyceum Theatre, and served as lecturer at moving panoramas depicting the Overland Route to India and the locale of the Crimean war. His claim to have been a schoolboy chum of Charles Dickens, made in a magazine published in Newburgh, New York, in 1875, has not been authenticated, but a letter written to him by Dickens in 1843 establishes that they were then acquainted. Stocqueler left the Northumberland Street business, one step ahead of his creditors, to serve as press agent in the United States for the giant new steam vessel, the *Great Eastern*. While in America he covered the Civil War for the *New York Evening Post*. Having reputedly declined an invitation to become professor of elocution and English literature at Columbia College (now University), he returned to England in 1864 and died at Brighton in 1885, aged eighty-four.

son, later Lord Lyndhurst, three times lord chancellor. How he acquired them is not known. That his affairs at that moment were in the hands of the bankruptcy court was, no doubt, neither here nor there as far as the Major Murray case was concerned.

Humphreys then returned to the subject of Sleigh's questioning, Roberts's putative association with Major Murray. Roberts's son added to what he had already deposed: He had heard that his mother and father met Mrs. Murray at the Surrey Music Hall, an auditorium at the Surrey Zoological Gardens in Lambeth, where the conductor Jullien had led huge orchestras, Thackeray lectured on "The Four Georges," and the celebrated evangelist Charles H. Spurgeon preached to overflow audiences. (This building had burned to the ground six weeks earlier, on 11 June.)

They also met her at the Crystal Palace, but the witness could not say how often. "Mrs. Murray came to my father's office about a fortnight before this occurrence." After supplementing earlier statements about his father's penchant for indoor target practice ("I certainly thought it was an odd place to fire pistols," he confessed), Roberts was allowed to stand down. He had, said the reporter for the *Morning Post*, given his evidence "with remarkable coolness and self-possession," even when being sharply questioned by both counsel.

John Singleton Copley Hill testified to the disorderly state of Roberts's rooms and further to the occasional use of them as a shooting gallery. He said he once took up one of Roberts's pistols and finding that it was loaded, proposed to draw it. "Don't do that—fire in the grate," said Roberts. Hill did so. The coroner: "That was a very extraordinary mode of discharging a pistol." Hill: "Yes, and I said so at the time, when Mr. Roberts said he frequently did so, and the people ran up on one occasion, thinking that a suicide or a murder had been committed." Under further questioning, Hill suggested that Mrs. Murray's dealings with Roberts et al., whatever their nature, had tended to induce hard feelings among them. "In fact, I had not been friendly with Mr. Roberts for some time in consequence of Mrs. Murray. I saw a lady outside the door and he told me I had insulted her. When he came out and told me I had insulted her he was angry, and I laughed at him. I saw them afterwards at the Crystal Palace, and he asked me what business I had there. I said the Palace was free for any man in England."

Mr. Canton, the surgeon who had extracted the bullet from Murray's spine, was recalled. After describing the wound, he endorsed the theory that Murray had indeed been shot from behind, and by a "steady, cool, and collected" person. That the major had inflicted the wound on himself was, he said, "within the range of possibility, but not at all probable. I have tried [one hopes with an unloaded pistol], but I could not do it." It would appear to have been a mode of self-destruction available only to a despondent contortionist.

His testimony was interrupted halfway through when Humphreys rose to announce that he had just received a note saying that young Roberts "has stated in the presence of several persons that he never saw Major Murray before this occurrence." When Canton left the witness chair, Roberts was recalled and, under questioning by Humphreys, said, "I remember going up to Major Murray's bed [on the day of the assault], and seeing Mr. Ransom there. Major Murray never asked me if I ever had seen him before, and I did not reply, 'Never in my life.' I saw Mr. Chatterton, a pupil in the hospital, at the same time, but I did not state in his presence that I had never seen Major Murray in my life, nor words to that effect. Upon my solemn oath, I have never said so to a living soul."

Whereupon Henry Ransom was recalled. He deposed: "I took young Mr. Roberts up to Major Murray's bed, and said, 'This is Mr. Roberts's son.' 'Which Roberts?' he said. 'Roberts, of Northumberland Street,' I replied. 'Is that his son? Then, he ought to be hanged, and his father killed, for shooting a man when he was on the ground.' Major Murray then said to Roberts, 'Do you know me?' Roberts replied, 'No.' 'Have you ever seen me before?' Major Murray asked. 'Never,' Mr. Roberts replied. The major then requested Mr. Roberts to state if he had ever heard him talked about, and Roberts replied, 'Yes, I think I have heard my father speak of you once,' and when asked what his father had said about him he said, 'Nothing.'"

Sleigh cross-examined Ransom at length, but he stuck to his story. Percy Chatterton, the medical student, corroborated his version of the meeting. Then Sergeant Golden "deposed that he asked young Mr. Roberts whether he knew who the person was who had been shot and escaped, and he said he did not. He added that he was reading a book at the time the occurrence took place, and several persons afterwards asked him if he knew anything of the man who had escaped, and he replied that he did not know him. That was before Mr. Roberts was taken to the hospital. When, however, young Mr. Roberts returned from the hospital he said he knew the person well; that it was Major Murray, and that he and his father had dined with him and Mrs. Murray about three months before at some hotel, and that some monetary transactions had taken place between his father and Major

Murray to a large amount." And so it was Roberts's word against the three witnesses'.

At this point the inquest wound up for the day. "The inquiry as it proceeds," ended the *Morning Post*'s report, "appears to excite the public interest more than ever in this extraordinary case—the cause of the fatal encounter, despite the mass of evidence which has been adduced, being still involved in the deepest mystery. It is, however, expected that some revelations which may tend to elucidate it will be made in the examination of a witness not yet produced, and to whom at present we need not particularly point." Its appetite thus piqued, the public had to endure a day without news. Because several jurors had other business, the inquest did not resume until Thursday.

(Vidil)

For the second week in a row, the Monday morning newspapers featured their editorial writers' reflections on the two cases as they had, by then, developed. The *Morning Chronicle* suggested, as we have seen, that the image the press had thus far painted of the baron might not be the right one. The very ambiguity that enveloped the man was enough to keep the public gaze fixed on him, even if his immaculate respectability was a myth. But this was an issue to which English justice was blind. Foreign-born parvenu or not, he would be judged fairly. Airily quoting Pope and Sterne, the writer opined that young Vidil's position was understandably awkward. But "life is very frequently only a choice of evils, and it certainly appears the lesser evil of the two for a son to permit a parent to be guilty of a crime against society and escape with impunity, than to be what serious people would call 'the humble instrument' in, as it were, adjusting the halter round his father's neck."

The editorial then pointed to several puzzling aspects of the case that had not been explored in the proceedings to date. It was crucial to establish what weapon the father used, for this would help determine whether the assault was a spur-of-the-moment affair (a riding whip, a ready weapon for any horseman if the handle were weighty enough) or coolly premeditated (a leaded stick, which would have had to be brought along for the occasion). Again, why propose a visit to the Duc d'Aumale and then miss the road the baron supposedly knew so well? And just how badly injured was the son? Cringing in terror at an old woman's knees, "he, nevertheless, possessed sufficient equanimity and presence of mind to endeavour to screen his father by giving a false account of the occurrence, and saying that he had been thrown against a wall." Readers were cautioned not to leap to any conclusions while the evidence was still so incomplete; but they might rest assured that, regardless of the eventual decision, the baron would be punished: "The doors of the Jockey Club and of the Travellers' Club will assuredly be shut in his face, even if the doors of Newgate are not closed behind him."

The *Standard*, after the customary disclaimer of any desire to prejudge the case, devoted its leader to the omission in the existing machinery of justice to which the brief session on Friday called attention: the lack of an official charged explicitly and exclusively with undertaking the prosecution of criminals. Numerous offenders escaped exposure or punishment because their victims, or even disinterested citizens with a sense of civic responsibility, were reluctant to get involved—to waste whole days in the company of policemen and in attendance at police courts, to have their names in the newspapers, to subject themselves, in some circumstances, to actual danger. Thus young Vidil's decision was perfectly natural: "We do not expect from any Christian youth the stoic Roman virtue to be the witness in chief to charges which might condemn a parent to death or to penal servitude. . . . Our boast is, equal justice to all in England, and a fair and open examination and trial. But there is a chance of that vaunt proving idle in the case under notice, and all through the want of a necessary public officer." They ordered things better in Ireland, where there were crown solicitors who did the work of a public prosecutor.

When the hearing was resumed on Monday, William Sleigh had a busy day. In the morning he represented Roberts's family at the first session of the inquest at Charing Cross Hospital, and in the afternoon he appeared on behalf of Baron de Vidil at Bow Street. In the latter place, five witnesses corroborated, in all essential details, the story already on record of what happened on that Friday afternoon three weeks before in the Surrey lane. These witnesses were John Evans, formerly identified as a bargeman, who now called himself an "engineer" residing at Twickenham railway station; Julia Fitzgibbons, spinster, aged sixty-two, the woman the bloody-faced Alfred clutched, crying, "Oh, protect me, mother! help me, mother"; John Tanner, landlord of the Black Dog public house at Twickenham; John Everett, private watchman for the Duc d'Aumale at Orleans House, who was sitting on a stool outside the Swan Inn when the two horsemen rode past on their way to his employer's house and when, some minutes later, they returned separately, without their horses; and Alfred Clark, the surgeon who had treated young Vidil. Tanner and Everett testified that the baron told them that his son had stood up in the stirrups, causing his horse to shy and throw him against the wall; Evans and Clark said that the son, in the presence of his father, had told them the same thing. Clark told how he had washed and dressed a star-shaped wound on his forehead and a similar one on the left side of his head, near the back. Both could have been caused by an instrument such as the knob of a whip. The lack of scratches on his face and of other injuries was inconsistent with the notion that he had fallen to the ground. The surgeon had sent the elder Vidil from the room on several occasions and in his absence had questioned the injured man further, but Sleigh intervened to prevent his telling what answers he had got. They were, in any event, such as led him to consent to the youth's plea that Clark's assistant return to London with him.

Young Vidil was again called to the stand. This time he allowed himself to take the oath, but the progress this concession indicated was illusory, for he again refused to testify.

The magistrate decided that the evidence provided in the written complaint and by the witnesses just heard warranted the case being sent for trial. He denied the baron's renewed application for bail, "because persons with ample means in cases like the present would be willing to make any sacrifice in money to evade the law."

After the proceedings ended, the baron left the court for Newgate prison; he seemed, said one reporter, "greatly affected and astonished at the result of the investigation." An incident that occurrred as he was being placed inside a cab did not contribute to his composure. Members of the crowd pressed forward to catch a glimpse of the accused nobleman, and the police had much difficulty in keeping them back. As the baron took his seat and the cab was about to start off, the crowd surged forward again and forced open the door. After considerable delay, the police freed the cab and it was able to proceed to Newgate.

They also arrested one John Crowther, a street hawker who had refused to stand back when ordered to do so. The newspapers described the print he had been peddling in front of the Bow Street court. No more veracious than any other such piece of street iconography, it purported to show the by now celebrated assault and was, they said,

> remarkable for its consistent inaccuracy in the main features and in all the details. The figures have evidently been drawn by some

one who has never seen either the baron or his son, though it must be admitted that the portrait of the former is not much more unlike him than any other person. This cannot be said of the counterfeit presentment of the young man, who, moreover, is represented with moustache and imperial, which he does not wear, and without whiskers, which he does wear. The youth is represented as tall, and of large frame, whereas he is small and slight; and the father is made much smaller, though, in fact, without being a tall or big man, he has considerably the advantage of his son in height, muscular development, and apparent strength. The inaccuracy is kept up in matters of costume. The baron, who, as the public are already informed, wore a white hat, being represented with a black one; and the youth, who wore a black one, appears with a white one. Bad as the original was, the prisoner deserves some credit for an artistic addition, having drawn with red paint an irregular streak descending from the young man's temple to his coat sleeve, and supposed to indicate blood flowing from his wound.

Crowther was haled before Magistrate Corrie the next day, in a courtroom suddenly quiet and empty. The following dialogue took place:

CORRIE: "Why, you are an old friend of mine. You have been often here, I think?"

CROWTHER (bashfully): "No, sir; 'twarn't here, sir. T'other, sir. Bagnigge-wells-road, sir" (a laugh).

CORRIE: "Clerkenwell Police-court?"

CROWTHER: "Yes, sir. Only for sellin' some of these here things" (pointing to the prints, which the police had confiscated when they arrested him).

CORRIE: "Well, I think you are sufficiently punished by being locked up all night. You may go."

MR. BURNABY (chief clerk to the magistrate): "You know you are liable to a penalty for selling these things."

CROWTHER: "I sell 'em, sir? It was the printer sold them to me. I ain't sold those yet" (a laugh).

His stock was restored to him, and upon being taken to the jailer's room to give a receipt for his wares, he at once started to hawk them to the constables and prisoners waiting there.

In the same editions that carried this bit of light relief, several papers brought some comfort to those of its readers who were anxious for the baron's own ease. On being formally received into the care of the Newgate jailer, he had conferred with his solicitor, Mr. Wontner, about renewing the appeal for bail, as "the restraint of personal liberty to which he had been subjected appeared to be very irksome to the baron. The public is aware," the *Times* said, "that prisoners before trial are allowed many facilities that are denied to them after conviction, and although the gaol regulations are very strict, still it may be as well to state, that under the present arrangements the baron will not have to undergo any degrading association with other prisoners." The application was once again denied, this time by the chief justice, and the baron's trial was set for the session of the Central Criminal Court to begin on the nineteenth of August.

(Murray)

The weather was oppressive in London when the inquest on Roberts resumed on Thursday, and the Charing Cross Hospital's board room was, said the papers, "almost unbearable from the heat." The windows repeatedly had to be opened to admit fresh air and then closed again to exclude the ceaseless noise of traffic in the Strand. But the spectators who packed the room willingly sacrificed comfort for the sake of being present as the moment of decision in this mysterious case approached.

The first witness called was Preston Lumb, the civil engineer who occupied the rooms over Roberts's. He too had heard the shots, as described by previous witnesses, but in addition "several strange noises, such as would arise from a heavy instrument striking a mattress or soft substance." They were, he said, "peculiar, dull noises" of a kind he had never before heard from below. But then a client entered his room, and he thought no more about it until he heard a cry of "Murder!" and went out to find young Roberts on the stairs.

Inspector Mackenzie reported that in his formal examination he had forgotten to mention one matter. Shortly after Roberts's death, he was at Major Murray's bedside when Superintendent Durkin and the two surgeons, Skegg and Canton, appeared. Canton said, "A person in whom we have taken some interest has gone on from bad to worse." "By Jove—died, has he?" exclaimed the major, seeing through the surgeon's euphemistic and superfluous effort to soften the blow. He then asked whether a clergyman had seen him with regard to his future prospects and was told that one had.

Young Willie Roberts was recalled, and under Humphreys's questioning admitted that he and another youth had gone to Liverpool

Messrs. Skegg and Canton, the Surgeons Who Operated on Major Murray.

three months ago with the intention of going abroad. He had with him the tidy sum of forty pounds, which counsel suggested was stolen; Roberts, however, insisted that the money was his, drawn from a savings account he had at the Camberwell and Dulwich Bank near St. Giles' church. His father had followed him to Liverpool and— not "brought" him back, as Humphreys phrased it, but "asked me to come back." He denied that he had booked passage on an outward-bound ship and could not remember the name of the hotel where his father found him or what street it was on. If Humphreys failed to prove he was a thief, he cast doubt, if not on the youth's character, at least on his memory, which had purported to be so positive and accurate in the last session. Humphreys adverted to his earlier statement to the police that his father had told him he had dined with Major and Mrs. Murray at a hotel, perhaps the Grosvenor, some time in the past.

"Did you tell the officer when it was?"

"No, sir."

"Then he must have imagined it when he said it was three months ago?"

"I might have said so, but I do not remember."

"Why did you not tell the coroner all this before?"

And the wretched youth took refuge in the timeless answer to such a question: "He did not ask me."

Now came the moment toward which the press's insistent cry of "Produce the Woman" had steered the public's expectations. Mrs. Murray (as we will follow the newspapers in naming her, without the gratuitous indignity of quotation marks) was called, and, said the *Times*, "the excitement among the crowded audience to hear and see her became more intense." She came into the room accompanied by a friend and was seated at the foot of the table. The *Illustrated Times* reporter gave the fullest description of the costume she had chosen for the occasion.

> Mrs. Murray [he wrote] was elegantly dressed in what appeared to be slight mourning. She had on a white bonnet, trimmed with black; a black veil, white muslin dress, with a small black flower pattern, a richly-figured black lace shawl, and black kid gloves. Her hair, which is of a golden-brown colour, was arranged, not in the prevailing mode, but in a manner evidencing a taste of her own, and no doubt adopted after mature consideration as most suitable to her face. Her complexion is fair and clear; her features small and tolerably regular, though conveying rather the idea of weakness.

It is evident that this reporter was less than favorably impressed by what he took to be an air of calculation in the young woman's dress and demeanor. "After casting a glance round as if to gather from the expression of the faces of her audience what amount of sympathy she might expect in the ordeal she was about to undergo she drew her veil down, but raised it again on the Coroner politely intimating that, thus muffled, her voice would not be heard sufficiently."

The *Times* reporter was markedly more sympathetic. Perhaps he and other spectators were well disposed toward the fair witness because she reminded them of another lady who also held disputed title to a married name—Theresa Yelverton.

> She was dressed plainly but very well, in the ordinary walking dress which would be worn by a lady of means and position. She wore a thick black veil over her face, and appeared to be in such a

Miss Anna Maria Moody, Known as Mrs. Murray

dreadful state of nervous agitation as with difficulty to keep herself from fainting or going into hysterics. Her distress was so
deep that it was quite painful to look at her. When asked by the
coroner for her name she replied, after an effort at self control,
with the question, "Must I give my real name?" The coroner said

it was certainly necessary that she should do so, when she said, in so low a tone of voice as to be all but inaudible, "My name is Anne Marie Moody." The coroner then said he must request her to raise the veil, which almost entirely concealed her face. After a minute's hesitation she did so, and disclosed the features of a remarkably pretty woman, apparently 25 or 26 years of age. [Another estimate placed her age at nearer thirty.] When all eyes were directed on her she began to cry, and became still more agitated. One of the medical gentlemen connected with the hospital stood by her, and when overcome, as she frequently was in giving her evidence, administered *sal volatile* and water, or gave her salts to smell. She gave her evidence in a low tone of voice, but with an evident effort to be clearly understood. At times, however, when referring to Major Murray, her hysterical attacks overtook her, and she made an effort to conclude her statement in gasps that were almost unintelligible, till she entirely broke down.

The man from the *Illustrated Times* was unmoved by the hysterics of a pretty woman under severe stress. He wrote that "she gave her evidence at times in a very agitated tone, at others with great coolness, and a rather affected prettiness of manner, which left a rather unfavourable impression on the mind." Whatever the effect of her performance might have been, she was present to offer information, and the coroner proceeded to elicit it.

Her name, she said, was Ann (or Anna or Anne: different reporters spelled it differently) Maria Moody, and she lived at Elm Lodge (or Cottage: again they did not agree) in the suburban village of Tottenham. She had formerly lived in St. John's Wood, which all present in the room would instantly have identified as a London neighborhood much favored by mid-Victorian gentlemen who could afford a discreet home away from home.

The Coroner: "Do you know Major Murray?"

Witness: "Yes" (bursting into tears).

"Did you ever see Major Murray and the deceased together?"

"No, never, never, never!"

"Do you believe they ever spoke together?"

"Never. I am quite certain of that."

"Do you think Major Murray knew the deceased by sight?"

"No, I am certain he did not. Wait,—I have made a mistake. He did know him by sight."

What she meant, it transpired, was that the major had once seen

Roberts but did not know who he was. Roberts, on the other hand, had also seen the major and did know who he was. She had been there when their paths had momentarily crossed, an occasion she would later describe. She had known the major for six or seven years and had taken his name five years ago; she had occupied the cottage at Tottenham since April or May of the preceding year. The major sometimes stayed with her but might also be absent for as long as a month at a time.

To the cost of all three, she had known Roberts for the past three or four years. Their acquaintance had begun when, on the advice of a friend who had gone to him on a similar errand, she applied to him for a loan. She had just had a child, and since she had already put the major to much expense in that connection at a time when he had other heavy bills, she did not wish to burden him with the additional fifteen pounds she owed. "I borrowed the money," she said, "to save the Major's pocket." Roberts allowed her fifteen pounds on a bill of twenty pounds at three months. ("If any moneylenders were present," remarked the *Illustrated Times* reporter, "they must have felt rather uncomfortable on hearing the suppressed groan that ran round the room when Mrs. Murray stated the terms on which she had borrowed the £15 of Roberts—125 percent.") Two months after the initial loan, she found she could pay only the quarterly interest out of the major's allowance to her. "He said that I should not make myself uneasy about it, that if I would be his he would forgive the whole of it." ("It was with the utmost difficulty," one paper reported, "that the witness was able to gasp out this statement, and when she had done so she became fainting and hysterical for some time. The windows of the court as before were opened, and after a short while the witness recovered, and continued her answers to Mr. Sleigh, who put them with the utmost kindness and delicacy.") "I told him [Roberts]," she said, "I was honourably intended to pay him the money, and that I was honourable myself, and I hoped he would treat me honourably." Quarter after quarter passed, and all she could do was continue to pay interest. Roberts had her in his toils, in the classic tradition of Victorian melodrama. She could not tell the major that she had gone to Roberts for money rather than to him. Roberts, she said, "held such awe over me that I was always fearful to displease him, feeling he might make my home unhappy."

And so, during these several years, Mrs. Murray visited Roberts frequently—first in Northumberland Court, where he had his office when she got her loan, and for the past year and a half at 16 Northumberland Street, to which he had moved.* She stayed, she said, for an hour or so at a time, leaving between six and seven in the evening. (This, it will be noted, varied materially from Willie Roberts's account of her comings and goings.) The visits, she insisted, were always of a "business" rather than an "intimate" nature, though it is hard to see why even an hour at a time was insufficient for her to pay her interest and for Roberts to make out a receipt—assuming, of course, that she paid in cash. At some time or other he suggested that they go to Scotland together for a fortnight or three weeks, a proposal she indignantly refused.

Roberts was nothing if not persistent. Knowing she liked music, he took her several times to concerts at the Crystal Palace. Repeatedly he expressed a wish for her to meet his wife. "The first time," Mrs. Murray recounted, "I refused to visit his wife, as I told him it would not be a proper thing for me to be sitting with his wife, and he there thinking of me and not her; and also that, as I was not married, it would not be a proper thing to do." (Supposedly it was he who had assured her where his thoughts would be at such a moment. One wonders whether Mrs. Murray's voice contained a tinge of irony.) But eventually they did meet. Roberts gave her a ticket to one of Spurgeon's revival meetings at the Surrey Music Hall. She went there with a friend, and "to my surprise I saw him sitting in the next seat to me, with his three children and his wife." She did not describe her feelings, nor speculate on Mrs. Roberts's. (How did Roberts introduce her—as a valued client of his who sometimes came round once or twice a week to pay her quarterly interest?) Nor did she say what the sermon was about.

The infatuated moneylender continued to observe and pursue her. It was in the course of this surveillance that he and the major once were within hailing distance of each other. "About two years since," she testified, "the major and I were walking down past the Horse Guards. We went down Victoria-street to the new railway bridge over the river [behind Victoria Station]. We stood there and saw them raising some of the iron work. We then came back by the river side, the same way as we had gone, and the major put me into an Atlas om-

*If Roberts had occupied the suite in Northumberland Street for only the past eighteen months, this would not seem to have been time enough, even in air-polluted London, for the front-room furnishings to have acquired the thick fur of dust that so fascinated the newspaper reporters. If the objets d'art were, in fact, worthy of a connoisseur, perhaps Roberts inherited the room in its present state from a previous tenant and, for some reason, never tried to sell the museum pieces, let alone dust them.

nibus at Charing-cross. That was about four o'clock. About a week afterwards I went to the deceased's chambers on business, and he said to me, 'So you can walk about town with gentlemen who don't choose to offer you their arm.' I replied, 'I walked with no one who was ashamed to offer me his arm,' and if he had seen me with any one he had seen me with the major. He then said he had seen me with a gentleman—I think he said on the Monday—go down past the Horse Guards, that he watched us to the corner of the Abbey, and that he saw me go into a house, meaning the second of four houses built by the Abbey. He said that he then took a cab and remained in it till we came back again. He said he first saw us again as we were crossing the road by the hotel, that he allowed us to pass him, that he got out of the cab, followed us to Charing-cross, and there saw the major put me into the Atlas omnibus. He said—'I then followed the major to 33, Harley Street.' That was all that passed about that."

The Coroner: "Had you been into a house?"

"Oh, dear, no; we walked past the houses by the Abbey."

"Then you had not been into a house?"

"Oh, dear, no; not any at all."

Another year passed, and Roberts was still spending cab fare to spy on his lovely debtor and her protector. Two months after the Murrays had set up housekeeping at Tottenham, she was returning home from an errand in the village when she saw Roberts pass in a hansom cab. "I still walked on. I then looked behind me, and saw him going into a shop. He was out in an instant. I went home, and was certain it was him, and felt anxious, and thought it would be the better plan to go up to town directly, and, if I found him at home, to beg of him to desist following me; and if he were not there to put my name on a piece of paper and put it in his letter-box, thinking that would prevent him from coming down again. Just as I was coming up, he came rushing up the stairs, and said, 'I've just had a 15s. ride after you,' but he could not find me; that it was too bad of me not to give him my address, and that I need not think I should ever lose sight of him, for he would never lose sight of me."

Roberts's state of mind that these incidents reflect could help account for his unlimbering of firearms. "He once told me," said Mrs. Murray, "that he might use them if I annoyed him. He said, 'I have pistols in the other room, and if you were to annoy me I might use them.'" Still, he had not expressed any ill feeling toward the major, let alone uttered any threats. The Coroner: "Do you know of any object that the deceased had in getting Major Murray out of the way?"

"Oh, he had a motive; he wanted me." Agitated though she was, she must have said this with some pride. Not every young woman could boast so devoted and persistent a suitor.

These, then, had been the long-term relations between Roberts, the woman in the middle whom he was able to control over an unpaid debt of twenty pounds, and the major, who knew nothing of her anguished situation. Several weeks before the fatal Friday, Roberts sent her a letter—which, like all the others she got from him, she immediately destroyed—asking her to drop into his office. He had learned, he said, that the Grosvenor Hotel Company needed forty or fifty thousand pounds. He had a client, Sir R. Anstruther, who had money to invest; was Murray's company really in need of such a loan? "I told him I thought there was some one who was going to advance the money, and if I heard anything more about it I would let him know."

"A week after that," she continued, "I went down to his offices and told him"—and at that moment she again became hysterical. A recess was called, the windows were reopened, and after she was revived she proceeded: "I went down to him and told him I thought they had obtained the money. He said, 'If you are not certain about it, I might as well see Mr. Anstruther;' and he then went out and came back in five minutes with a time table. He looked at the times the boats left from Boulogne for Folkestone. He said they were too late or too early for the baronet to cross. He was so anxious to see Mr. Anstruther that he would have gone away, if possible, that day, but he said he was so ill in crossing over that he could not undertake the journey. Before leaving he said to me, 'I met the major yesterday.' I said, 'Did you; where did you see him?' He said, 'We just got too late for the boat as it was starting from London-bridge, and I waited with him till the next boat arrived. We both went up [to Westminster] in the same boat, and got out at Hungerford-bridge. He walked up in front of me into the Strand. I saw him make his way along Pall-mall.' He then asked me whether that was his usual way of coming to town, whether he came by train or by omnibus? I told him he generally went up by boat, but that he came up to town by train or omnibus. He then asked me if he had got the money, and I said, 'You ought to know business matters better than I do. If I were you I would go to the secretary.' He said, 'Oh no; that won't do, for he would get the benefit of advancing the money; and if I advance it I ought to have it.' I then said, 'Then, why not go to the board?' He said, 'No, that will not do. If I were to write to the major and ask him to come to my chambers, do you think he would come?' I said, 'If I were you I would write to him, and he will answer your letter.' He then said, 'Supposing I go to the club to see him, do you think he would see me?' I immediately begged him not to do so, but suggested he should write to him, as he would be sure to answer his letter by return of post. He then asked me if the major had taken me out anywhere since I had been at home. I told him we had not been out, but we were going on the following Monday to see Blondin."

On Wednesday, 10 July, two days before the fatal meeting, Mrs. Murray again visited Northumberland Street. "He asked me if they had obtained the money. I told him that I was nearly certain that they had. He said, 'I have seen Anstruther, who is most anxious to lend the money.' I was then going to leave, when he said, 'What a hurry you're in; can't you stay a little while?' I said, 'No, I have to pay a visit to a friend.' He said, 'I saw you with the major, with your little child and nurse, on Monday at the Crystal Palace.' I said, 'I don't think it could have been us that you saw; where on earth were we sitting?' He then described exactly the position where we were sitting. I said, 'How was it I did not see you? Surely I must have seen you if you were as close as you say, for I was looking through the glasses.' He said, 'Oh no, your little child had just run away, and your nurse had gone after her to fetch her.' I felt a little annoyed with him, and said, 'What could have induced you to have gone down there that day when you knew I was going there?' He said, 'I went with my wife,' and, I think he said, 'my sisters. I took tickets for them in the reserved seats; thinking that all of you would be sure to be there, I thought it would be better for me to remain outside.' Before I left him he asked me when the next meeting of the board would take place, and I told him the same time as before. He asked me when he should see me again, and I said, 'I do not know.'"

Nor did she realize that by verifying to Roberts the major's customary route from London Bridge to the Strand she had set up her lover for the bill discounter's felonious attentions, and inadvertently, but by poetic justice, ensured that she would be rid of Roberts himself, the man who had turned a twenty-pound bill of acceptance into a prolonged nightmare. "He knew that I loved and idolized the major. He knew that our happiness depended on him, and he made me miserable."

"Major Murray has always treated you with affection and kindness?" asked Humphreys.

"He has always treated me in the most noble-hearted manner that any man in the world could possibly do," she replied.

"And is his disposition amiable and kind?"

"It is."

"The witness then retired," the press reported, "amidst some manifestation of applause," one old gentleman, "no doubt smitten with the lady's charms, making a great demonstration with his umbrella." After a brief adjournment for refreshment, the inquiry resumed. Three letters from Mrs. Murray were then submitted in evidence. The ink was faded, and the handwriting was so fine and delicate that they were not always easy to decipher. The first two read:

Five o'clock, Tuesday.

My dear sir,—This very minute I have received your kind letter, and, believe me, from my very heart, my feelings are at this present time inexpressible. Your pretty expression that "some day far hence my little treasure (and indeed she is a treasure) may step in and ask the same favour," is indeed true. And good is it of you to make every one happy about you, more especially those you love. My dear sir, as regards the present for my baby what can I say sufficient to show my perfect heartfelt thanks. Could you be in the dining-room of 48 [her former address in St. John's Wood] quite quick, and when, as I now am, then, perhaps, excuse the tears of gratitude and love that are now dropping one by one from my eyes. I assure you I cannot express my heartfelt thanks for the pleasure that your note has given me. In fact, when I first sat down to write this I fancied I could have filled sheets of paper with love to you, but somehow I now seem that my thoughts are checked, and I can only wait to lie my head on your shoulder and cry tears of joy (not unmixed with sorrow) for the many happy days I have passed with you. I [You?] shall hear when I receive the "parcel," of course.—Ever yours,

Annie

Wednesday Morning,
a Quarter before Ten.

My dear sir,—It is utterly impossible for me to express my thanks for the truly elegant presents you sent my darling baby last evening. The elegant cloak, the charming robes, and the darling little bonnet are of the most costly description, and again I must say that words can but feebly express my gratitude. They reached me last night a little after ten, and, believe me, I could not sleep for thinking of them. Oh, how pretty my pet will look in that darling little bonnet, so purely elegant. And then the caps, too—the most perfect little gems of things I ever saw. I can but look at her in them, and yet in my heart I should like my pet baby to be able to look at them years hence and see your presents, and for them to be as fresh as ever; but I hope she will live to see them, although discoloured by time, and thank you far more graciously than her mamma can now find herself capable of doing. Let me see you, and I will then be able to say more; at present I am hardly quieted down. The idea of your thinking of my little darling has quite taken me aback; and may you, my dear sir, have as many happy years in store for you and your family as we have spent days together (I think you will then have reached fourscore years), is the sincere and heartfelt wish of yours truly,

A. M. Murray

The third letter by contrast was a model of businesslike terseness.

Tuesday

Mr. Roberts—Dear sir,—As I have four places in Parliament-street [where the offices of the Grosvenor Hotel Company were located] to view the procession of the Queen to the Houses of Parliament, and it's more than I require, I thought perhaps some of your family would like to use them. I will be at your chambers to know the result by 12 o'clock.

—Yours obediently,
A. M. Murray

Mrs. Murray perhaps meant to repay Roberts for the favor of a ticket to Spurgeon's service. Evidently she had no qualms about meeting his wife again; and, in fact, Mrs. Roberts was present to see the queen pass by.

Also handed in as evidence was a fourth letter, unsigned but in Roberts's handwriting:

Saturday

If I am still in "anger" in your mind can you forgive me?

If the expression of yours, "you know when you are treated in a gentlemanly way" was not leveled at me, I should be pleased to know this. I do know that my folly did me out of what has by this been a great loss.

You hold my destiny, and if your anger stands, then I know but one in life to look to.

This will come to you early on Monday.

If you will bring your olive leaf, say by two o'clock, you will brighten that which is now gloomy.

No one sought, and no one offered, an explication of this *cri de coeur*.

These letters were discovered in the course of Inspector Mackenzie's patient search through the chaotic heaps of documents in Roberts's rooms. The last was found, torn up, in the grate in the back room. Mackenzie also had put together, from scraps scattered on the floor, a draft of an undated letter in Roberts's handwriting:

Monday

May you never experience two nights and a day such as that I passed through,—the sad, the just punishment for my wickedness in truth I call—for me to attempt to say why or wherefore the act sprung into existence is wholly without my comprehension. Could I feel that you put me back in your mind free from the recollection of what I might say it would be especial joy. I must build upon your coming to hear you say—"How very sorry I am to learn the cause of your absence, but trust it will pass away with the least possible harm." I am almost fearful to express a wish lest it should be doubted after my absurd folly, but could you look within and read, I would not fear the scan, nor trouble about grieving during the search. Never again shall such a thing spring from me, and if you can by any means send me a line that will tell me of my full reinstating with you, do it; if any angry thought towards me is still in your heart, out with it; do not retain any but the cheering one. I have often heard from you; how to win you— what I want to feel; my mind follows on the last attempt; but this, I dare say that, be it as it may, there's not one that lives on earth that can lay claim to being more honest and faithful in their love towards you than I. The folly of Saturday may have caused you some annoyance, but [   ] describe my torture of mind [   ] and say why have [   ] thus the almost causeless [   ] rehearst the circumstances I could [   ] believe it true. I have doubted it having occurred;

the time between now and Saturday will droop on. I was looking forward to it; I hope, though, not with anything of what I fain would hear; but now it will pass by with this crushing remembrance, coupled with the knowledge of who is claiming you in all ways.

No attempt was made at this point to associate this lengthy and somewhat incoherent venting of contrition with Roberts's relations with Mrs. Murray. But it must have reinforced the developing image of him as a honey-penned womanizer.

Mrs. Murray was now recalled and examined by Sleigh:

"Look at this note and tell me, madam, if you can recollect the date when you wrote it. It is about some presents to your children?"

"Not children—child."

"I beg your pardon."

"It was written about two and a half years ago."

"How long had you known Mr. Roberts then?"

"I had known him then about twelve months."

"Then it was about ten months after he had made that very disgusting proposal to you that you wrote this letter. Was it written from where you were then residing?"

"Yes, from St. John's Wood."

"And am I to understand distinctly that after Mr. Roberts made this proposal to you you continued your visits to him at his chambers?"

"Yes, and I will tell you why: Mr. Roberts was so mistrustful of me he was always watching me; and if ever he saw me out he thought I refused to go to his chambers because I preferred some one else, and I wished to make him think that if I wanted any recreation I would as soon go and talk to him as to any other person of my acquaintance."

"But your own feelings were rather against him?"

"At first I was awfully disgusted with him."

"And that disgust did not decrease in intensity?"

"Indeed it did not."

"Have you ever passed days with him happily together?"

"No, not days."

"Well, hours then, enjoying his society?"

"Oh no, there was nothing of that sort between us."

"You never felt delighted to be with him?"

"No."

"Allow me to read a passage in this letter:—'I can only wait to lie my head on your shoulder and cry tears of joy (not unmixed with sorrow) for the many happy days I have passed with you.' In the first place, I ask you, is it not a fact that you passed many happy days with him?"

"No, I never passed a happy day with Roberts. He had sent the presents to my child, and I was over-delighted, and I wrote that on the moment."

"Then do you mean to state that the passage is not true?"

"It was craft on my part. I wrote to him so because I had not paid all the money off, and I knew that if I did not write in this way he would annoy me in some way. I was obliged to him for sending the presents to the child, but I would rather have been without them."

"Then I will read you this passage:—'Could you be in the dining room of 48 quite quick; and when, as I now am, then, perhaps, excuse the tears of gratitude and love that are now dropping one by one from my eyes'—and you write to him, 'my dear sir.'"

"Yes. He used to say if I would only say 'dear' to him he would be satisfied; but that I spoke to others more warmly, whilst I spoke to him coldly, and therefore I used the word 'dear.'"

"Now listen to this. You say—'I assure you I cannot express my heartfelt thanks for the pleasure that your note has given me. In fact, when I first sat down to write this I fancied I could have filled sheets of paper with love to you, but somehow I now seem that my thoughts are checked.' That, too, is all craft, is it?"

"It is."

Sleigh "closed his eyes, shrugged his shoulders, and sat down with an air of most virtuous indignation, intimating that after *that* he would not ask her another question."

Humphreys took over: "You say you have been constantly in fear of Mr. Roberts?"

"Yes; he was constantly wanting me to leave my home entirely, and to go abroad with him."

"Did he send carriages for you at times?"

"He used to send carriages for me at times, and letters to say at what time the carriage would be there; and I did not know what on earth to do."

"Look at this letter [the one beginning, "May you never experience . . ."]."

"This is the draft of a letter which he sent me three weeks since."

"Did he always write to you in terms of affection such as that?"

"Not always."

"Were you in the habit of using the term when you wrote to him, 'Ever yours, Annie,' with a stroke under the 'Annie'?"

"Oh yes."

The exploration of the discrepancy between Mrs. Murray's alleged hatred and fear of Roberts and the warmth of her written sentiments ended at this point. The production of the letters seemed to have cooled the spectators' sympathy for Mrs. Murray. As the second round of her examination ended, there was no demonstration as there had been after the first, even from the venerable gentleman with the umbrella.

The coroner and his jury now moved from the board room to one of the hospital wards to take Major Murray's testimony, the medical men having decided that he was not yet well enough to appear in open court. The press described his appearance: between forty-five and fifty years old, about five feet ten in height, with light blue eyes, brown hair, whiskers, and mustachios. He looked pale and weak, and his throat was so heavily bandaged that he had difficulty moving his head. Sitting at the end of a table along which the jurymen were ranged, he took the oath, repeating "So help me God" with "marked emphasis." His firm tone and the clarity with which he spoke convinced the newspapermen that "he was speaking the whole truth and nothing but the truth."

"My name is William Murray," he began—at last his given name was divulged! "I live at 33, Harley Street, and at Tottenham. I was a Major in the 10th Hussars. I know a little of what has passed in the court below, but not much, for I have seen no papers." In the testimony that ensued, he went over ground already familiar, adding some matters not previously divulged. On their way from Hungerford Market to Northumberland Street, he said, he had repeated his statement to Roberts that he had no power to act for the hotel company in respect to the proposed loan. Roberts said he understood that, but wished to learn more particularly what the firm required. "There is one thing I must ask you at once. Do the directors intend to give any personal security in addition to the security of the building?" "I said," Murray went on, "'Certainly not; beyond our individual stock we will give no security whatever—mine happens to be rather a heavy one.' He said, 'Oh, yes, I understand you are one of the largest shareholders in the company.' I said, 'As to that, one gentleman is a larger shareholder than I am, and there are many gentlemen who have as many shares, but I believe I am safe in saying I am one of the largest shareholders.'"

By this time they had arrived at Roberts's office, which Murray once again stressed he had never before entered. After Roberts excused himself to go into the front room, "I looked round and thought it the most extraordinary place I had ever seen—torn-up papers, bottles, broken picture-frames, all lying about, a most disreputable looking place. He almost immediately came back into the room and took a seat at the table immediately in front of me. He took a pen in his hand and said, 'I should be glad to learn what interest you propose to give.' I said, 'I am not in a position to say, but I would hear what your client is prepared to take.' He then said, 'Oh, I understand the offer is to come from us.' I said, 'Certainly not, sir. Under any circumstances we should not give more than five per cent.' He said that would do very well, and I then said, 'Now, would you favour me with your card of address?' He said, 'Immediately'—got up from the table and walked round to a desk sort of place there was there, and began rummaging amongst the papers. I thought he was looking for his card-case, and took no notice of what he was doing. Presently I felt a slight touch on the back of my neck, heard the report of a pistol, and dropped off my chair on the ground." It became more and more evident that in Murray the bill discounter had caught a Tartar. Once more he related, blow by blow, what had ensued. Previous versions, relayed through intermediate parties (Ransom and Mackenzie), had conveyed the savagery of the encounter, but to this ferociousness Murray, speaking directly to the jury, the press, and eventually the world, added an exuberant delight in recalling how, despite his own serious wounds, he had reduced his antagonist to a mutilated, blood-soaked wretch cowering in a corner.

Murray then threw new light on those moments at the window overlooking the yard. Clay and Clark had "called out to me not to get out of the window, that they would come and open the door for me. At first I was inclined to let them do so, but on second thoughts it struck me that men who could hear pistol-shots and take no notice of them—who would listen within a few feet of their heads to such a fight as had been going on—must be in league with the murderer; so I did not choose to trust them." A Titan of physical strength, Murray was also a cool customer. "When I was shot I did not scream out. I never tried my voice, and it was lucky for me I didn't. I recommend you, if you have to fight for life, to fight in silence; don't waste your time in talking."

Sleigh: "I trust I never shall have to fight for my life, and hope this is your first [he did not add "last"] fight."

"It was my first fight in an attempt on my life, but I was out in the Crimea, ready to fight if I were wanted. When I threw that thing [a metal flowerpot, first mentioned in his present testimony] at him he said 'That won't do, Master William.' When I was hitting him on the head with the tongs he said, 'Come, come, give me fair play—fair play!'" It was rather late, one thinks, for either combatant to invoke the rules of chivalry.

In the course of his testimony, the major introduced a small detail not previously on record. Sergeant Golden, it will be recalled, said that he had been passing through Northumberland Street, on the side opposite Number 16, when he heard the first cries of murder. He had then seen the major emerging from Number 15, through which he had passed from the back yard. But Murray now said that when he reached the sidewalk, "I saw a policeman standing on the opposite side of the street, and I called to him to go into the room up stairs and take charge of a man who had been murdering me, and he said he could not. He said he was watching the house, and he had sent for assistance." Although Clark, Clay, and Ransom were with the major at that moment, none of them reported any such reply or conduct on the policeman's part.

Murray now completed his testimony—it had required an hour and a half, and at the end he seemed tired—and the jury moved back to the board room. An official of the Grosvenor Hotel Company deposed that the major was one of its ten directors and that Roberts had never attended a meeting of the company. Four other medical students gave identical evidence to support testimony already heard: that at the major's bedside young Roberts had distinctly denied ever having seen him before. Humphreys offered to call "many gentlemen of position in society who can come forward and speak to the Major's character and demeanour from his infancy"—he must have been a veritable "Mars in swathling clothes," as Henry IV called Hotspur—but the coroner said that as this was only an inquest, character witnesses could be dispensed with.

Roberts's widow, clad in deepest mourning for the husband she had buried on Friday, was then called, to repeat the conversation she had had with Major Murray on the afternoon when she and her son arrived at the hospital. The gist was essentially as previously reported: Murray denied he had ever seen Roberts before, but she told him that he was known to Roberts, who had often spoken of him to her. She had been in Mrs. Murray's company three times: at Spurgeon's service, the queen's opening of Parliament (since the vantage point for the procession was the offices of the Grosvenor Hotel Company, one wonders why the major was not present), and the Crystal Palace.

This concluded the taking of evidence. In summing up, the coroner offered to read over the whole record of the proceedings, but the jury said that this was unnecessary, and the coroner limited himself to the deposition Murray had just given.

Without leaving the room, the jury reached a unanimous verdict of "justifiable homicide, committed by Major Murray in defense of his own life." The room erupted with applause. The coroner thanked the jurymen for their great attention and for deciding the case as he would himself have done, and Superintendent Durkin, having been thanked for his assistance, expressed the hope that the compliment "would be extended to Inspector Mackenzie, who had acted most judiciously and zealously in unravelling this case, which at first appeared mysterious, but which he trusted was so no longer." (Applause.) Major Murray, back in the ward, was informed of the verdict, and his police guard was withdrawn. There is no record of what occurred when he and his loyal mistress were reunited.

Mrs. Roberts was appointed administrator of her husband's estate, but because the lease of his rooms from the Catalonia Cork-Cutting Company had not yet expired, the wrecked furnishings remained *in situ*. There seems to be no record of Madame Tussauds' trying to buy them for a veracious reconstruction of the scene in the Chamber of Horrors—a name that, had anyone thought of it, might have been most appropriately transferred to the rear room in Northumberland Street.

Major Murray was released from the hospital in early August and went at once to the family home in Harley Street. His convalescence was impeded by an exfoliation from the vertebra where Roberts's bullet had struck, but on 13 November the *Times* was able to announce that after Mr. Canton, who remained his physician, removed the offending piece of bone, he enjoyed a complete recovery. And he did indeed. The robust constitution that had enabled him not only to survive Roberts's attack but to repay him at a fatally high rate of interest continued to serve him well. He lived to the great age of eighty-eight, dying on 28 March 1907 at Ossemsley Manor, Christchurch. What happened to Anna Maria Moody, called "Mrs. Murray," we unfortunately do not know.

Only ten days before the coroner's jury rendered its judgment, the press had, almost with one voice, denounced Major Murray's fantastic story as utterly unbelievable. Now it had perforce been turned into a corps of true believers: the testimony had left it no choice. Without overtly eating crow, each newspaper had to concede that the verdict was the only one that could possibly have been reached. "It is a masterly Verdict," said the *Sun*, "a manly, resolute Verdict, which by its exceeding simplicity and distinctness reflects honour upon those twelve honest Englishmen." "It will be seen," said the *Morning Herald*, "that the original statement of Major Murray has not only been borne out, but received as the literal truth by those whose duty it was on their solemn oath to judge impartially. It can no longer be doubted, we think, that in one case, at least, the wilful and deliberate perpetration of murder has been followed by instant and condign retribution. . . . The unhappy, misguided fatalist, cursed with judicial blindness, and the victim of his own impious folly, would hardly venture to hatch another crime in view of his yawning grave, and so was silent. Never was vengeance more speedy or more commensurate. It may be a scandal to the law, but it will not be inconsistent with the aims of justice if villany so deep-dyed and so deliberate never fail of a like reward." There was something reminiscent of Greek tragedy in the spectacle of a would-be murderer becoming the agent of his own destruction.

Only the *Sun* professed itself to be entirely satisfied. Every vexed aspect, it said, "has been completely accounted for. *So* completely accounted for, so conclusively explained in every one of its particulars, that we believe it would be absolutely impossible for the jury to have found a more admirably truthful verdict than the one with which the Coroner's Jury yesterday brought the proceedings to a conclusion." But this was to take a restricted—a lawyer's—view of the case. The journalist's view, given scope by the example of imaginative fiction rather than confined within the rules of criminal procedure, continued to maintain that there was more in the Murray case than met the eye or was visible in the inquest record. The tangle of mysteries the newspapers had so sedulously merchandised since Saturday, 13 July, could not be so easily disposed of. Under the circumstances, they did not bear on the sole question the jury had to decide, whether the major killed in self-defense. But the testimony the coroner's jury heard was far from resolving a number of deliciously nagging questions of motive and behavior; instead, it raised several fresh ones. The *Sunday Times*, for instance, asked: Did Roberts inveigle Major Murray into his chambers with malice prepense, or was his attack the result of a sudden impulse? Was the proposed loan to the Grosvenor Hotel Company a fabrication? Answer: "Roberts deliberately contrived the opportunity of murdering Major Murray; and all the talk about a projected loan was but an ingenious portion of this device. For Roberts had previously been informed by 'Mrs. Murray' that the loan was being obtained in another quarter." A further question: What was the true nature of the relationship between Roberts and Mrs. Murray? "Was the lady bound to him by wicked intimacy, or only by nervous subjection? Here, again, we strongly incline to give absolute credence to her own statement on this point."

The *Daily Telegraph* was not so sure about this and other conclusions its contemporaries were reaching. In what was probably the most masterly and provocative review of the case, it undercut its approval of the verdict by adopting an ironic stance: "Circumstances which may for years remain a judicial puzzle to very wise heads were all as clear as the sun at noon day to the twelve respectable gentlemen who assembled in the board-room of Charing-cross Hospital."

> Major Murray will issue from the hospital not only a free man, but with a reputation for energy and determination which may be hereafter, and in certain circles, of considerable advantage to him. Bill discounters will, in future, be wary how they engage in pecuniary transactions with his mistress, or how they solicit him to visit their chambers for the purpose of contracting loans. The Major has proved that a stout pair of tongs and a well-wielded wine bottle may laugh powder and ball to scorn, and that a man with two bullet wounds in his head is more than a match for another previously unhurt, and with a whole arsenal of pistols at his side. We cannot say that we rejoice at this verdict, but we nevertheless unhesitatingly accept it. . . . But may we be pardoned for making a slight confession? We cannot exactly understand the grounds on which the jury arrived at their verdict. It may be that we are obtuse; that we are dull of comprehension; that we cannot put this and that together; that we have no experience in unravelling the mysteries of crime; that we are not versed in the intricacies of "crowner's 'quest law." . . . It is not invidious, it is not churlish, it is not libellous on our part, we trust, for us to take the verdict of Thursday last with a "reservation"—that reservation being merely that the evidence given on the inquest contains some very strange discrepancies.

This, continued the editorial writer, despite the major's last statement, "so explicit, so lucid, so borne out even by the few broken and incoherent sentences alleged to have been uttered by Roberts."

There is, indeed, a candour about the Major's mode of expressing himself, a precision of technical picturesqueness in his narrative of the affray—how he passed from the tongs to the iron flower-pot and jug, then to the wine-bottle, and then to the tongs again—how he battered his opponent's head while he lay on the ground and under the table—how he hammered him across the wrists to disable him—which can only be equalled by his exclamation of "By Jove!" when he was told that the man he had beaten had ceased to live; by his telling the widow of the slain Roberts that "she was as mad as her husband;" and by the remarkable piece of worldly wise advice he volunteered, when asked why he did not cry out, that "when you are fighting for your life, it is as well to fight in silence and not waste your breath."

The paper congratulated itself for having sagely prophesied, at the outset, that there was a woman at the bottom of the mystery—a hypothesis of which, as it happened, it was not the sole proprietor. It applauded Mrs. Murray for having steadily declined Roberts's "dishonourable proposals."

Adoring and idolising the Major as she did, Mrs. Murray refused; *but* she did not decline to accompany Roberts to one or more places of public resort; *but* she consented to accept from the amorous bill discounter caps, mantles, and other presents for her baby; *but* she wrote him several letters, couched in the most affectionate strain, thanking him for the presents, and signing herself Annie. May we ask if Mrs. Murray accepted her bills of exchange as "Annie"? In these letters she spoke of "gratitude and love" to Roberts, and of the "many happy days they had spent together." . . . Mrs. Murray said that "she never meant a word of them," and that their composition was all "craft," to prevent Roberts from letting Major Murray, of whom she stood in great fear, know of the money matters between them.

All this took the bloom off Mrs. Murray as the very personification of innocence and victimization.

The termination of Mrs. Murray's evidence was met by some applause in the court. But for that calm confession of hypocritical deceit in her correspondence with the dead man—but for her easy avowal of "craft"—we should sympathise with and join in that applause. Of course we believe every word that has been uttered by Mrs. Moody Murray. Can Roberts rise from his grave to say that she was faithless to her paramour? Of course we agree *toto coelo* with the verdict of the intelligent jury, but we must, nevertheless say that the whole affair is a very strange one, and that we cannot even now comprehend its various mysterious phases.

The *Examiner* took the view that when she applied for that fifteen-pound loan to close the books on her confinement, Mrs. Murray had no idea what a Pandora's box she was opening at the same time. Perhaps she was an innocent flirt, "thinking to practise not very wickedly on the infirmities of the little bill-discounter until she ended in the fascination of a terror at the fierceness of the unsatisfied passion she had roused. Then her thought must have been *'Fulmineo spumantis apri sum dente petita'* [a wild pig in his rage breeds fire in the tooth]. But the tooth of fire was for the man who stood between her and his greed for her."

A judicious modern reader may wonder why Mrs. Murray did not take the simplest way out of her captivity, by taking one of the toylike pearl-handled pistols and shooting Roberts. There was, after all, legendary precedent for such a course, in familiar woodcut illustrations of real-life murders which depicted a beautiful woman standing over a man's body with a smoking pistol in her hand; and female murderers (or suspected murderers) would soon become heroines of certain sensation novels. Victimized or not, the woman with the weapon—if firearms were too difficult for a sheltered wife or mistress to manage, there was always poison—was an established figure in fact and fiction.

Or, if the forthright alternative was too unfeminine, why did Mrs. Murray not simply screw her courage to the sticking place and confess to the major what she had done? There would have been the classic tableau of a kneeling woman pleading for her master's forgiveness, as the repentant Guinevere begged King Arthur's in the poem Tennyson had published two years earlier. If one can extrapolate from her catalog of the major's virtues, understanding and forgiveness would have descended upon her. However strapped he might have been when she needed the fifteen pounds three or four years ago, he evidently was now in no need of money; he was a principal stockholder in the Grosvenor Hotel Company and could afford a snug retreat for the two of them in Tottenham. And had she not told Sleigh, as she finished her gruelling appearance before the jury, that the major "would never refuse me any money I wanted"?

But this solution, it seems, was more ideal than practical. The

Sunday Times's reflections on Mrs. Murray's situation may not have taken into account the particular relation that existed between the major and his mistress—the possibility of a genuine love that transcended the stereotype of a mere terminable sexual arrangement cemented only by the cash-payment nexus. But they throw significant light on the status of women in the mid-Victorian period, and not only in the eyes of the law:

> She confesses that she stood in awe of [Roberts]. And the hold that he had upon her was a much more formidable one than a thousand innocent people will be able to appreciate. They will say, why did she not tell the major when she found how grossly her creditor was abusing her. The exact moment, however, when that bold step should have been taken most likely went by before the danger in which she stood was realised; and the revelation of her peril had been ingeniously anticipated by the completeness of her actual subjection. For it should not be forgotten that a mistress stands in all such cases as these on very different ground from that which a wife would occupy. The frank confession of an embarrassing predicament by a wife would in itself be taken as a proof of innocence; coming from the lips of a mistress, it would be much more likely to occasion distrust and indignation. Moreover, a wife is rendered bold by the consciousness that, in any ultimate dispute, the law will come in to her protection; whereas, a mistress must be incessantly tormented by the knowledge that she can hold on to her lord not a moment longer than his own confidence and sympathy endure. At the instigation of the merest caprice of jealousy, she is aware that he may leave her to a fate all full of helpless misery and hopeless dishonour. Her timidity, therefore, is the exact proportion to the slightness of the chain by which she is bound to the comforts and privileges of her life.

Other papers treated "the woman question"—or "the woman *in* question"—more lightly. "For once opinion and rumour hit upon the right reason as if by instinct, and that reason is one almost as old as creation," said the *Morning Herald*. "Our readers will guess at once, if they have not been forewarned already, that the first and last cause of this horrible tragedy was no other than that which of old, and in Homer's song, joined two continents in hostile conflict." The *Sun* concluded its brief editorial on a positively flippant note: "Wonderful as this singular tragedy is in every particular, it is perhaps most wonderful in the circumstance that it affords a literal verification of the truth wittily expressed in that quaint old verse of Quevedo:

> 'Tis said a Justice of the Quorum,
>   Who was no fool
> When theft or murder came before him,
>   Made it a rule
> At once to stop the lawyer's chatter,
>   Saying, d'ye see,
> "Let's probe the bottom of this matter—
>   WHO IS SHE?"

Although none of the other papers were as vigorous as the *Daily Telegraph* in pursuing the unresolved threads of the case, each had its own reservations. "Not . . . every point connected with the mysterious tragedy is yet cleared up," said the *Daily News*, "or perhaps now ever can or will be. But the main and hitherto missing clue of its explanation has probably been supplied." The *Morning Post*, while concurring in the verdict, added that it was "far from satisfied" with the evidence and "cannot help surmising that there remain some facts still undisclosed." The writer accepted Murray's story, rejected Roberts's meager and unconvincing one, and regretted that Mrs. Murray's evidence did not help clear up any vital issues. What bothered him was the "most trivial motive" alleged for Roberts's actions. "Here is the motive assigned for one of the most cold-blooded and determined attempts to commit a murder which have been made in modern times, and which, even if it had been effected, could by no possibility have realised the object which dictated it. We now leave it to our readers to determine whether our conjecture is not a plausible one, that there remains something which has not been disclosed." With this dark hint, the *Morning Post* rested its own case.

The *Times*, by contrast, took the high road, stylistically as well as in chosen theme. It did not hesitate over any inadequacies of motive or evidence, nor did it find any profound societal message in the story. Instead, it pondered the moral significance of Roberts's self-destructive quest, "the romance of uncontrolled passion."

> Ninety-nine people out of a hundred [it began] would be perfectly happy if they could make up their minds to do without some one thing which they particularly desire to have. It is unnecessary, after the Northumberland-street inquest, to say what,

or rather who, was the one great object in the late Mr. Roberts' scheme of happiness, the absence of which converted all the worldly comforts and success of a prosperous middle-aged bill-discounter into gall and bitterness, and finally precipitated him into chaos.

"The most coarse, degrading, and vulgar affair that can be conceived" was an affront to the very concept of romance ("great, refined, and sublime"), and "the end of all was the tragical death of the most impassioned, enthralled, romantic, demoniacal, atrocious, and miserable of all bill-discounters."

FRIDAY, 26 JULY– FRIDAY, 23 AUGUST (Vidil)

With the Northumberland Street business out of the way and the Vidil case awaiting trial, the press had to mark time and, in the absence of hard news relating to the latter, keep the public interest alive by other means. On Wednesday (24 July) the *Daily Telegraph* virtuously announced its decision to let justice take its course: "We have no desire to comment upon De Vidil's case. The man is committed for trial; comments or surmises as to his innocence or his guilt must, after this unavoidable mention of him, be both objectionable and superfluous; and henceforth we shall leave him to his gaolers and his judge and his jury, until he is granted a good deliverance or otherwise at the Old Bailey. After that event our functions as assessors of the decision may recommence." And so its Vidil editorial for the day was devoted to a smart attack on Sir George Cornewall Lewis, the home secretary ("the guardian of the public peace of the country") for his apparent dereliction of duty.

It may be that the Home Secretary, remembering that the Baron de Vidil had once been connected with the glove trade, and adding to it a much quoted aphorism bearing on the Emperor Napoleon, imagined that the Baron had only forgotten to put on his glove when he hit his son with a hand of iron. When we were occupied day after day in uncoiling the halter from about the neck of Dr. Smethurst, it was thought in many circles a most ungenteel thing to save a man from the scaffold who had been so solemnly sentenced to death by the Lord Chief Justice; and this chariness of meddling with a nobleman bearing one of Louis Philippe's titles may be due to a similar feeling. Different views were entertained when old George II, refusing to pardon the murderer Lord Ferrers, exclaimed, in his broken English, "He has done de deed of de bad man, and he shall die de deth of de bad man."

Other newspapers, lacking the *Daily Telegraph*'s resolve, continued to comment directly on the case. The *News of the World* the following Sunday was not satisfied with the alleged motive for the attack on the young Vidil ("If the object was so mercenary, a man of the world would scarcely resort to a country ride and an attack by a whip handle": poison was more favored by the avaricious, at least in Victorian England) and deplored the youth's obstinate silence: "Why? 'I understand that my father has made some kind of insinuation against me; if so, I must tell all.' What is meant by all?"

The *Observer*, too, worried about what had become by now preeminently the case of the reluctant witness. To this writer, it was a clear-cut instance of obstruction of justice.

> The magistrate threatened to send him to prison if he did not give evidence, and this course would in all probability have had the effect of opening his mouth; but it was suggested by the Baron's legal advisers that the health of the young man was so delicate that confinement would probably put it out of his power to appear at a subsequent examination, and that if he were given up to his friends it would be more likely to further the ends of justice— a plan the best calculated, as it turned out, to befriend the Baron, for his son was subsequently more than ever determined to hold his tongue. No one can fail to sympathize with the feelings of Mr. de Vidil under such trying circumstances, but if conduct like this were to be sanctioned, how could justice be administered?

Citing a recent election bribery case at York in which a key witness who refused to testify was imprisoned for four months before he changed his mind, the *Observer* concluded with a ringing affirmation: "Justice should be administered to all alike, and . . . the laws should not be defeated in deference to the feelings of a youth who refuses to give evidence. . . . The law, to be respected, must be equally applied in all cases to all persons."

The next day (5 August) the *Times* opportunely fanned the smoldering embers into flame by printing "additional facts which have been obtained from a source on which the fullest reliance may be placed." The first "fact" was startling enough: it was young Vidil who had been the aggressor, not his father. The baron, to be sure, had been much annoyed by his son's refusal, without giving any reason, to stop and dine with him at Hampton. But when they arrived in the lane, "either by accident or design the young gentleman struck his father somewhat sharply with his riding whip. The consequence was that the baron, under the influence of momentary excitement, struck his son two severe blows on the head with the butt-end of his own whip, but he had no idea that he had inflicted any serious injury upon his son," who was of "very weak and nervous temperament." His subsequent journey to France had nothing to do with the incident. Far from regarding himself as a fugitive from justice, as soon as he learned that a charge had been made against him in England, he went to the procureur-général, who told him that "although there was no treaty that would justify his extradition, and there was no intention on the part of the French government to give him up, still it was suggested that he had better leave Paris." While the government was considering the matter, the baron, placed "under temporary restraint," "expressed his determination to go to England to meet the charge, whatever it might be, that was made against him, and he made a personal application to the Procureur du Roi to that effect." It was only upon arriving in England, in the custody of two French policemen, that he learned that his son had accused him of a capital crime.

With similar show of authority—and these assertions were to be borne out by testimony at the trial—the *Times* clarified the financial aspects of the case. According to the marriage settlement of the Baroness de Vidil (née Susannah Jackson), the sum of £20,000 was vested in trustees who paid her the interest in her lifetime. Upon her death, the baron was to enjoy a life interest in the estate, and upon his death the principal was to go to whatever issue had reached the age of twenty-one. A further sum of £10,000 was bequeathed by Susannah Jackson's father to his grandson, Alfred. This money Alfred had already received. So, "the Baron de Vidil would have no interest whatever in this money, unless in the event of his son dying without making a will, or bequeathing it to him by such an instrument." Which is one way of putting it; another way would be to point out that by the death of his son the baron would, under the favorable circumstances mentioned, receive £30,000 outright. What the *Times* did point out, however, was a material fact attested to by a witness at the trial, a clerk to a firm of solicitors: in August 1844 the baron had sold his life interest for £4,800. Presumably he had been hard up at the time, seventeen years earlier. Was he again in financial difficulties? If so, the common assumption that he had attempted to kill his son for his money would have been considerably strengthened. But no such circumstance was to be suggested at the trial.

The *Times*'s revisionist version was widely copied, usually without attribution. Within a week it had appeared in the *Daily News*, the *Illustrated Times*, the *Observer*, and the *Daily Telegraph* (which credited the *Observer*). Other portions of the press, however, denounced this overly partisan exercise of journalistic freedom, which some interpreted as an attempt by the baron and his friends to undercut in advance whatever story the son might offer if he did finally agree to testify. The popular weekly paper, *Bell's Life in London*, fumed: "A more scandalous attempt to poison the minds of jurymen, who ought to come into the box free from all prejudices occasioned by mere *ex parte* statements, has seldom been made. It will not have any effect, but it is not the less censurable on that account. And in delivering his charge to the grand jury, and afterwards, in summing up the case, it is to be hoped that the judge will refer to and unsparingly condemn these attempts to corrupt the public mind and destroy that entire impartiality with which jurymen ought to enter on their important and often painful duties."

The *Observer* criticized the *Times*'s intervention more adroitly, in the form of advice to the imprisoned baron to consider "in what particulars his case will not hold water, and thereby giving him a few hints how to shape his defence." (1) If the baron had been annoyed by his son's refusal to stop at Hampton for dinner, and the disagreement was so serious as to lead to violence, it would have been more natural for him to have struck Alfred first. Instead, the allegation was that a disgruntled Alfred struck him first: for what reason? (2) When the baron came up to the old woman whom his son was clutching, he did *not* say (as truth, given his version of events, would have required him to say), "My son struck me by accident or otherwise, I do not know which, and I in the heat of the moment struck him again. I regret that the blow should have been so severe." Instead, he sought to exculpate his son by concocting the story that he had fallen from his horse and struck his head against a wall. (3) The baron's claim that he did not realize his son was seriously injured conflicted with the known fact that he sat up with him until midnight in Duke Street. "All we would recommend to the baron's advisers," concluded the *Observer*, "is to give a little more consistency to their allegations, as they may find that his last statements may not be any more credited than his first." And at the same time, his son should be made to testify. The public "will oppose any attempts to defeat the ends of justice, come from whatever quarter they may."

The *Illustrated Times* also declined to accept the *Times*'s revisionist tale. "We trust, for the credit of English justice simply," it said,

> that the grand jury will have a better idea of their duties than to attend to suggested defences raised only in the columns of a newspaper, or to throw out a bill because a prosecuting witness declines his evidence. . . . Young Vidil may, perhaps, not object, under certain circumstances, to have his forehead smashed; but what is it to us, even if he prefer that alternative to dining with his father at Hampton? The less he cares about it the more business have our authorities to interfere. We are not going to allow foreign gentlemen to carry on such amusements as this just because it suits their humours or conveniences. We in England have our rights and our interests in the preservation of the Queen's peace; and, if this be broken, somebody must pay for it, young M. Vidil and the chiefs of the Orleanist party notwithstanding. We have not the slightest prejudice in the matter, one way or the other; but . . . we want to know all about it—whether influential friends of any person concerned choose to tamper with a *Times* paragrapher and to procure the suppression of evidence or not.

Meanwhile, the baron languished in Newgate. "He does not appear so much affected by his confinement as would be imagined," reported the *Times*, "and during the last few days he has been visited by several persons of distinction, who seem to take the greatest interest in him, and to be strongly impressed with the conviction that he is entirely innocent of the crime of which he is accused." But that judgment rested, finally, in the hands of the twelve men, good and true, who would hear the evidence at the Old Bailey.

The grand jury having returned a true bill against the baron, his trial got under way at ten o'clock in the morning on Friday, 23 August. It was a government prosecution after all; two days after the *Daily Telegraph* attacked Sir George Cornewall Lewis for refusing to interest himself in the case, it had had to retract, and save face, as gracefully as possible: "The Home Secretary, it seems, has not finally refused his sanction for the prosecution of the Baron de Vidil. We have never been blind to the difficulties of the case, and do not wonder that Sir George Cornewall Lewis took time to deliberate upon the course which he should pursue." His seeming dilatoriness was all the more understandable in view of the fact that he was about to take up a new portfolio, that of secretary for war.

The indictment against the baron was composed of three charges, in descending order of seriousness: assault with intent to murder (a capital offense), assault with intent to do grievous bodily harm, and unlawful wounding. Sir Colin Blackburn (later Baron Blackburn) presided; this was one of the first criminal cases he heard as justice of the Queen's Bench. Associated with him was Mr. Justice Hill. The prosecution was conducted on behalf of the solicitor of the treasury by Mr. Clerk, of whom we know little, and Mr. Beasley, who in 1875 would appear for the crown in the case of Henry Wainwright, the East End brushmaker who was arrested while riding in a cab with luggage that contained the dismembered body of his late mistress.

The baron's defense was in the capable hands of Mr. Sleigh and Sergeant William Ballantine, a well-known figure in the criminal courts. He had led for the crown in the Smethurst murder case two years earlier, and three years hence, assisted by Beasley, would prosecute Müller, the railway murderer; still later (1870) he would lead for the plaintiff in Sir Charles Mordaunt's divorce suit against his wife, a trial memorable for the Prince of Wales's appearance on the witness stand, and the next year he would join Sleigh in representing the Tichborne Claimant in the first stages of that turbulent case. Some professed to recognize him in the character of Mr. Chaffanbrass, the courtroom performer who had enlivened the pages of Trollope's *The Three Clerks* (1858). Chaffanbrass, brusque, badgering, and wily, was about to reappear in the pages of the same novelist's *Orley Farm*, which had begun publication in monthly numbers in March.

Clerk made the opening statement to the jurymen, begging them to dismiss from their minds all they had heard or read about "this most painful and, in many circumstances, most extraordinary case"— a counsel of perfection, given the saturation press coverage it had enjoyed. He did not intimate the difficulty he faced in attempting to convict the baron on the charge of attempting to murder. Young Alfred's signed deposition, which had set the machinery of justice in motion, could not be used because it would have had to be affirmed by him in court, and apparently there was no prospect of this. Hence he had to depend on the testimony of witnesses, only one of whom had actually seen the attack—and he was incapable of appearing, being confined to his sickbed in the Twickenham cottage and repre-

Serjeant Ballantine, Leader for Baron De Vidil (From Horace Wyndham: *Judicial Dramas* (London, 1927)

sented only by the deposition he had painfully signed with his mark. Perhaps, though, this was a blessing in disguise; at least the absent Rivers could not be subjected to cross-examination.

The first witness was a hostler at a livery stable in Oxford Street, who testified that at the instruction of Baron de Vidil he had taken two horses to meet him and his son when they arrived by train at Twickenham. The son's horse was the quieter of the two, not requiring a whip. The baron's would sometimes stop and rear up.

Now came the much anticipated moment of Alfred's taking the stand. In an almost inaudible voice he was understood to say, "Am I called by the counsel for the defense? I object to being sworn by the prosecution. I must leave myself in the hands of the Court, but must decline to give evidence against my father." Mr. Justice Blackburn told him that a witness was not entitled to be concerned with the possible effect of his testimony. The youth remaining adamant, Blackburn conferred with his colleague, Justice Hill, and then repeated his admonition. Receiving the same answer, he asked Clerk if he required Vidil to be examined. Clerk replied that he certainly did. Vidil having uttered his refusal once more, Blackburn, stressing the gravity of such an obstinately uncooperative attitude, sentenced him to a month in prison. ("Sensation," reported the *Times*.) He was removed in custody, and the trial proceeded.

John Evans, the engineer at the Twickenham station, repeated the testimony he had given at Bow Street. Under questioning, he said that when the baron jumped the fence to the field leading to the river, he had in his hand a whip, "which appeared to be mounted with some metal at the end." He was shown the son's whip, which a detective offered in evidence, but said it was not the one he had seen in the baron's hand as he dived into the shrubbery. The baron rejoined Evans and Alfred at the Swan Inn no more than two minutes later. He had no whip at that time.

Julia Fitzgibbons, repeating her earlier testimony, said she had picked up a hat, riding gloves, and a whip near the spot where bloody-faced Alfred had clung to her. Subsequently she gave the whip to the landlady at the Swan. She could not describe it, apart from her impression that the mount was silver, nor could she estimate its size, because she did not measure it. (Laughter.) Counsel showed her the whip Evans had failed to identify, and she said it was longer than the one she had picked up.

James Tanner, the publican, and the Duc d'Aumale's watchman had nothing material to add to what they had contributed at the magistrate's hearing. Alfred Clark, the surgeon, was positive that the wounds he described could not have been sustained by falling against a wall but "might certainly have been caused by blows from some blunt instrument."

Alfred's uncle again identified the letter he had received from the baron reporting the "accident" and said that on the morning after the assault his nephew had stayed only about three hours at Ware House, leaving, he thought, before the letter arrived.

SERJEANT BALLANTINE: "This young man has always been of a peculiar temperament, has he not?"

PARKER: "I hardly know what you mean by 'peculiar temperament.'"

"Do you know that three or four years ago he was in confinement as a lunatic?"

"No."

"Has nothing of that kind happened?"

"I know that he was taken into custody in the Isle of Wight."

"And confined as a lunatic?"

"No, I believe not."

"Will you swear that? Was he not taken up as a wandering lunatic, and were you not telegraphed for as his next friend then in England?"

"I know that he was taken up at 12 o'clock one night."

"What for?"

"I believe from having taken some brandy and being unable to take care of himself."

"I repeat, was not the charge to your knowledge that he was a lunatic?"

"He was stated to be a lunatic, but I did not know that was the charge against him."

"It may have been for being drunk or for anything else; but in point of fact that was the imputation upon him?"

"Yes, there was such an imputation upon him in the Isle of Wight."

"His father was out of England at the time, and I believe you telegraphed to him?"

"Yes, I did."

"Did you inform the father what was the charge against him?"

"Yes."

"That he was supposed to be a lunatic?"

"I think I told him what I am telling you. When I saw the magistrate I asked him to let me take the young man under my care, and he consented."

"The young man had, in point of fact, caused a great deal of excitement in the island?"

"He may have done so. I immediately brought him over to Portsmouth and telegraphed for his father."

Clerk, the prosecution counsel, took over the witness again in an effort to limit whatever damage Ballantine's line of attack had caused. To his questions, Parker replied: "I have seen the young man constantly during the last four years. He left Cambridge immediately preceding this event at the Isle of Wight, which occurred about four years ago. At that time he had not formed any habits of intemperance, and since that time I have never seen anything indicating a wandering intellect. On the contrary, his faculties are remarkably clear, although he has some peculiarities of demeanour. I consider his intellects are not only clear, but singularly good, and I may say that he took a first-class at Trinity, and that he has since undergone an examination at college. He is rather fanciful about his health, and is fond of consulting medical men respecting it, but I know nothing about his labouring under a delusion. The only delusion he has is in respect to his health, if you can call that a delusion."

A solicitor's clerk produced documents to prove the terms of the marriage settlement. The bedridden John Rivers's deposition was read. Detective Sergeant Wilkinson testified that he had taken custody of the baron when his French police escort delivered him to Scotland Yard on 15 July. At this point, the prosecution rested its case.

After a short intermission, Serjeant Ballantine rose to outline the case for the defense. Like Clerk for the prosecution, he began by dwelling on the danger that the wide and prejudicial publicity the affair had received would imperil the chance of a just verdict, and entreated the jurymen to erase from their minds every scintilla of knowledge they possessed except that which would be supported by sworn testimony. "In the streets and shops of London," he said, "are to be found portraits of father and son, in which the father is pictured as murdering his son; and in the very neighbourhood of the court the indecency of such an exhibition is to be witnessed." Ballantine "protested against the supposition that the extraordinary course of proceeding that had been adopted by the son was in any way calculated to benefit [his father]; on the contrary, all those proceedings were calculated to injure him." (After the verdict was in, the *Observer* rebuked Ballantine for making the pro forma plea for utter detachment from the insidious suggestions of the press, a plea that was peculiarly inappropriate under the circumstances, although the press was more culpable than this writer admitted: "The learned counsel should have been the last man to talk about prejudices raised against his client, when the only discussion that has been raised in the public journals was instigated by the ridiculous defence put forward by the baron's own advisers in the newspapers.")

Ballantine then maintained that not the slightest bit of evidence tended to suggest that his client had any murderous intentions toward his son. The instrument used was a horse whip, scarcely a deadly weapon; the so-called assault occurred in a public thoroughfare, in broad daylight, and at a well-frequented spot where his cries might easily be heard and the assailant immediately identified. Besides, where would the baron have planned to dispose of the body?—a question also raised by at least two papers in connection with Roberts's difficulty in Northumberland Street. The injuries the young man suffered were so slight as to cause him "little or no inconvenience," and he was easily able to travel down to Hertfordshire the next day.

The greatest difficulty the father faced in making his own defense, Ballantine argued, was his son's contumacy. No one else could explain what were the true circumstances behind the sudden assault. Here the serjeant seized upon the theory that the *Times* had floated in its controversial article. "Supposing that the son had insulted the father, or that he had struck him, would he not have been justified in returning the blow? He begged the jury to bear in mind that he was not stating that this was the case—he was merely suggesting that it might have been, for it was beyond the prisoner's power to show what the real facts were [under the law as then written, the accused party could not speak in his own defense], and it was upon this ground that he stated that the refusal of the son to give evidence was not only of no benefit to the prisoner, but was calculated to injure him, and prevent him from obtaining that justice to which he was entitled." And so Ballantine returned to his earlier theme, at such length and with such emphasis as to suggest that it was the young man himself who was on trial. Vidil junior's silence seems, in fact, to have been the strongest card—albeit fortuitous—in the defense's hand. Ballantine hinted darkly that "If the son had been called as a witness, he [Ballantine] was instructed to have put certain questions to him of the most painful character, and he would ask the jury whether it was not natural, under the circumstances, that the baron should have been most anxious to prevent the affair from coming to the knowledge of the public." The victim's silence gave Ballantine a golden opportunity to dispense innuendo with a liberal hand, and he made the most of it.

The learned counsel concluded by saying that "he felt assured that the jury would not convict one of their own countrymen of any offense upon such evidence as had been adduced in support of the present charge, and that they would award the same measure of justice to the prisoner who was a foreigner."

A short procession of witnesses testified to the baron's good character. (At least one newspaper reported that they came from the bench, where they had been seated beside the two judges.) The Honorable George William Barrington, who was to succeed his father as the seventh viscount in 1867, deposed that the baron was "a humane, honourable, and well-conducted gentleman." Lieutenant-Colonel Tarleton said that he was "a gentleman in every respect. He is of a rather hasty disposition, and entertains strong political opinions, and sometimes he expresses them in rather strong terms." (Laughter.) Prince Demidoff of Russia described him as being "very humane, very social, and very honourable, incapable of committing a crime of this description." George Byng, seventh Viscount Torrington, former governor and commander in chief in Ceylon and present lord in waiting to the queen, characterized him as "a most kind, amiable, excellent gentleman," adding, "A great many of his friends I know are abroad at this time, or they would also have been here to speak to his character." The last character witness, who, somewhat to the embarrassment of counsel, volunteered his testimony, was a mere City shopkeeper, who recalled that he had known the baron when he was in business in the City and had bought goods—gloves or buttons?—from him. "I always considered him a very respectable and honourable man."

With this light anticlimax, the defense rested its case.

Mr. Justice Blackburn summed up. He was confident that the jury would decide strictly on the basis of the evidence presented in court and that the course taken by the prisoner's son would have no bearing on that decision. He then explained the difference between the several counts of the indictment, which involved the degree of the bodily harm suffered and the question of intent. That, according to the evidence, what the baron had in hand when he jumped the fence was no more lethal than a riding whip was a material point against the imputation that he meant to do grievous injury. And he did not think the jury should place too much weight on the likelihood that the property, under certain contingencies, would come into the baron's possession.

The jury retired and after twenty minutes returned with a verdict of guilty of unlawful wounding. Mr. Justice Blackburn concurred with the decision. In considering the sentence to be imposed, he said he would have been more lenient had the prisoner struck his son with the light end of the whip. But heavy end it was, and, though he was "sorry to have to pass such a sentence upon a person in your position"—class feeling could not be wholly expunged from the judicial system—"I cannot do otherwise than to order you to be imprisoned and kept to hard labour for the space of twelve months."

The prisoner, reported the papers, "appeared a good deal agitated when the sentence was pronounced."

Almost without exception, the newspapers issued that weekend concurred with the jury's verdict and the court's sentence. The *Sunday Times*, it is true, found fault with the form of the charge under which the baron had been tried. It was "difficult to understand how, under the circumstances, the prisoner could have been tried for wilful murder; but . . . still more difficult to perceive how, if murder were not his object, he could have been suspected of anything more than a common assault. Altogether, the result of this painful investigation may be accepted as an illustration of the anomalies which obtain in the interpretation and administration of our laws."

The *Daily Telegraph* endorsed the verdict with none of the reservations it had expressed when Major Murray was cleared of a similar imputation. The irony it had then employed was replaced by honest rejoicing. "For twelve months," it said, "[the baron] will have to give up the delights and luxuries of his clubs in London and Paris, for the chilling discomforts of a common gaol; for twelve months he will have no opportunities of seeking amusement and distraction amid the exciting pursuits of the turf, and certainly for the same length of time he will be utterly unable to take any more suspicious rides with his son in the solitary lanes of Twickenham."

One or two papers complained not of the anomalies in the legal system but of the sheer incompetence of the prosecution ("negligence," "otiosity and languor," and "carelessness" were some of the terms they used), which had resulted in the baron's being convicted only on the least serious charge. The weapon used in the assault was a crucial piece of evidence. But the whip produced in court had not been proved to have any connection with the case, and the one the old woman, Julia Fitzgibbons, found at the scene of the assault remained in the hands of the landlady at the Swan tavern. Was it not conceivable that the baron had climbed over the fence immediately after wounding his son for the sake of ridding himself of another weapon, perhaps a heavier whip, which he had secreted on his person? If so, why had the police not searched the field, especially the shrubbery between the fence and the river? "Had the case assumed the gravity of murder or manslaughter," said the *Morning Chronicle*, "the whip would have been found. It is the most culpable carelessness—and the blame for it must rest somewhere—that a search was not made for it, and that the whole case was not more carefully investigated."

Moreover—and here it was not the alleged incompetence of the police or the prosecution that was at fault, but the rigor of the law—at least one willing witness knew more than he was allowed to tell. Mr. Clark, the surgeon, had conversed with both father and son while both were agitated and the son supposedly talked freely in answer to his asking what had happened, but he was forbidden to recount what he had heard from young Vidil when his father was out of the room.

But it was the son's refusal to testify, a windfall that in many cases would have enabled the defense to come off with a total victory, that most engaged the editorial writers. What manner of man was he, anyway? The *Sunday Times* expressed no sympathy for the nonwitness. "If this miserable youth had held his peace from the beginning," it said, "he would either have won some glory for himself or spared much shame to his house. But he blubbered and blabbed in the moment of trial, and then, having made a humiliating compromise of his courage, made a still more deplorable compromise of his moral obligations."

Most of the press, however, took a kindlier view of young Vidil. "We incline to the belief that he has truly stated the grounds of his reticence," announced the *Morning Advertiser*, "and that he carries with him to prison the consolation that it is not from his lips that his father has been condemned." "The son is in prison," echoed the *Morning Chronicle*, "because he is forgiving and merciful—because he postpones the demands of public policy to the holy instincts of filial affection." The *Standard* took a severe view of Serjeant Ballantine's "straining his advantage"—Alfred's opportune silence—"to a point as cruel to the youth whose generosity had placed him in his power as it was unnecessary to the defence. . . . Justice has always her drawbacks and compromises, but it seems as though the goddess had lost more than her sight—her balance, when we see that this young Mr. de Vidil must be first half-killed by his father for the misfortune of finding himself under his protection on the Queen's highway, occupied in visits to Royalty; that he must then be punished by a month's imprisonment for his filial unwillingness to give evidence against him, and that, finally, he must be compelled to have it published by his father's counsel—an attack surely worse than the first— that he absents himself from the witness box because he is engaged in a conspiracy for his father's ruin, to which he is too cowardly to give more than a covert support!"

In the end, the *Daily News* decided, both men were losers. A year hence, when he finished picking oakum in Coldbath Fields, the baron could scarcely expect to resume his former position in society, and his son could not outlive the double stigma of imputed lunacy and the irresolvable ambiguity of his action, or inaction, toward his father. "The father has ruined both himself and his son; and the son, if actuated by spite, has done less injury to his father than he would have done by giving evidence; if he was actuated by parental [the writer meant "filial"] affection he has not succeeded in saving his father, but in either case he has at all events ruined himself."

Why, then, did he act as he did? Was it spite, for some undivulged offense, or a noble attempt to protect his father? If the latter, asked the

Times, why did Serjeant Ballantine not take his cue from Vidil's implied willingness to testify for the defense and put him in the box? Or was it fear of submitting himself to cross-examination, which might have revealed facts he wanted to conceal? And which man, father or son, would have been injured had those facts become public knowledge? Or would it have been both? "Rarely in this country," said one paper, "has a judicial trial, followed by conviction, thrown less light over the circumstances of a crime whose mystery had so long perplexed and interested public curiosity." The case, said another, "has received the practical solution which will sufficiently satisfy the unthinking crowd; but those curious on such topics will reasonably complain that we do not know, and most probably *shall never* know, the real facts of this cruel assault." Those facts, said a third paper, "are known only to two living beings—one of whom declines, and the other, by the law of England, is forbidden to reveal them."

No doubt clubland still supported a current of *on dits*, as the journalistic jargon elegantly called gossip. Perhaps—though the theory seemingly did not find its way into print—the curious delay in charging the baron (more than a week elapsed between the assault and the filing of the young man's "information") was attributable to the slow development of a conspiracy (if there was one) by Alfred's uncle to discredit if not seriously incommode the baron (if, with his cosmopolitan airs and habits appropriate to an intimate of French royalty and British aristocracy, he was persona non grata to his late wife's sturdily English family).

The *Daily Telegraph* eloquently summed up:

A dispute, we were to believe, had arisen between father and son, and it was of such a nature that neither wished it to be brought before the world. Must we rest contented with this vague and imperfect explanation, which seems to hint at some secret too foul and hideous to be brought into the light of day? It would appear so. We have no Poe amongst us now to penetrate this mystery, and arrive through a dark labyrinth of evidence and deduction at that mental standpoint where all becomes open and clear. And if we had, even his sagacity might be at fault. Perhaps, after all, we do not lose much by the absence of more explicit information than we now possess. We should see nothing, it may be, that would benefit us to look upon, if the veil were completely raised upon the motives and actions of these two men. Rumour may whisper as it pleases, and hiss its dark stories into our ear, but we will pay no heed to them. We have done for the moment with both father and son. There is a cloud hanging around them; whether it will some day burst into storm, or pass quietly away, none of us can tell. But behind that cloud both must for awhile be hidden from the world, lost amid the gloom their own acts have cast upon them. Whatever the position of the young man, though it may be a misfortune which no deed of his has deserved, the very name he bears is dishonoured, and a stigma attached to it which it will take many long years to remove.

If anyone was prepared to shed light on the secrets that tantalized the press and public, it should have been Serjeant Ballantine. But in his desultory memoirs, published many years later, he declared that he "learned no more than the rest of the public, and the events leading to the transaction remain still a mystery. Vidil was very well known in French society, and the circumstance of my defending him introduced me to the acquaintance of many of its members. They could give no clue to the transaction, but I fancy for some reason he had previously been in ill odor."

In mid-September, Alfred finished his term of imprisonment in Newgate. Although his offense was such that no labor was required, the relatives who came for him found him "pale and in ill-health"— perhaps more so than when he was sentenced. At that very moment, Madame Tussaud's announced the display of "a full-length portrait model of the Baron de Vidil" in the celebrated "chamber of Comparative Physiognomy," better known as the Chamber of Horrors. The baron himself remained in Coldbath Fields, a notoriously severe prison; at that time (19 September) the *Times* reported that he was "employed daily in picking oakum," a hard penance for his sin. When he was released the following July, however, the same paper said that he had been "chiefly employed in mat-making." At least he had been spared that most unproductive of all forms of Victorian prison exercise, walking a stated number of hours each day on the treadmill. After his release, he went to Paris, where he died on 20 April 1868. His son survived him by many years, dying at St. Leonards on the Sea, a favorite valetudinarian and retirement community, on 21 March 1899.

CHAPTER THREE

The Press Responds

Every murder of true stop-press quality led Victorian editorial writers to study the nation's image in the red-misted mirror of crime. Indeed, an industrious student could compile from the newspapers' commentary on the dozen most celebrated Victorian murders a valuable anthology of contemporary psychological and social opinion. Although the twin sensations of the summer of 1861 did not qualify as murders, they evoked more than the ordinary spate of editorial interpretation. Only a week after they leaped into the headlines, the *Spectator* (a journal of opinion, not a newspaper) reported, correctly if a bit cynically, that "the press teems with moral but singularly stupid reflections on the soundness of a civilization amidst which crimes so horrible can occur. The public, horrified, but excited, accepts the condemnation as a sort of expiation for the interest it cannot but feel, and without troubling itself with analysis, declares the contents of the newspapers [that is, the crimes themselves, not the press coverage] a 'disgrace to the nineteenth century.' The unmeaning phrase will be repeated some thousands of times in the course of next week, and then the usual glorification of the age will recommence once more."

On a day-to-day basis, the prime attraction of the two cases was the set of mysteries each presented. Initially these were simple questions of fact springing especially from Major Murray's unbelievable tale, though even before the provable circumstances began to be sorted out there was much freewheeling speculation on the motives of both Roberts and Baron de Vidil. Once the "facts" were spread on the legal record, the press was satisfied on the whole, though several papers continued to murmur darkly about some that still had not come to light. But mysteries of motive remained, albeit a somewhat different set from those that had been uppermost in the early stages. And throughout the active life of the two cases they sometimes were enlarged into riddles of general significance, part moral, part psychological, part social.

Who could, after all—borrowing a phrase late twentieth-century Americans remembered from a classic thriller series on the radio—properly read the evil that lurked in the hearts of men? Like at least one other paper, the *Daily Telegraph* found a guidepost for its thinking in Thomas De Quincey's celebrated essay, "Murder, Regarded as One of the Fine Arts." De Quincey, it said, called attention to

> the necessity of showing how foolish and futile are the common endeavours to make out a regular sequence of motive and action, applicable alike to all natures, and tending as surely to one particular end as the needle points toward the pole—as the idle apprentice's act of playing chuck-halfpenny on a tombstone indicates his direct and inevitable progress to the gallows. Mr. William John Roberts might have pursued his useful and unostentatious career of money-lender, without so much variety of incident occurring as to raise him for one brief hour into the region of romance, and have died full of years, in which case nobody would have been put to the trouble of speculating on those phenomena of his existence which are brought into open discussion by the violence of his end. People would have contented themselves with paying him the usual civilities which are thought to be due to the dead, and he would have passed into respectable oblivion as an exemplary citizen, an affectionate husband, a kind father, a faithful friend, and ever so many noble characters beside. If we were to philosophise about all such persons among our daily acquaintance, we should have enough to do. . . . Mr. Roberts, we dare say, had his occasional detractors in this harsh world; but the most candid of them all would scarcely have predicted for the Northumberland-street bill-discounter a lot so dramatically retributive as that which has befallen him. However, here is the body of Mr. Roberts lying, fearfully disfigured, in a lower room of Charing-cross Hospital; and the problem for our consideration is, how did he come to such a pass?

The *Daily Telegraph's* answer, vindicated in the event, was the easy one of Find the Woman. It remained for the *Times* to turn Roberts's unpredictable end into a moral homily derived from the "two excellent precepts" in Ecclesiastes: "Be not righteous overmuch" and "Be not overmuch wicked." Two types of men, it argued, violate this ethical golden mean by their inability to "do without some one thing which they particularly desire to have." The so-called "righteous man" "pursues what is called a great idea, which is to regenerate society and effect nobody knows what. If you ask him for the proof of the correctness of it, indeed, he has not much to say; but that is neither here nor there and does not signify; it is 'a great idea.'" This misplaced idealism may render him "simply an egotistical fanatic and an intolerable coxcomb, but [not] with his set of admirers, who think him an angel." The ill-fated Roberts belonged to the other category. Far from being an idealist of any stripe, he was

> a coarse, brutal fellow, who first takes a mean advantage of an unfortunate woman coming to him to borrow money to force his affections upon her, for which she, even in her situation, has moral feeling enough to rebuke him. . . . At the bottom of the whole [story] lies one powerful, absorbing, and uncontrollable passion. It is . . . perfectly easy for a man to enjoy the society of his neighbours and all kinds of common-place pleasures so long as he has no other particular craving to haunt and agitate him— no tormenting want, nothing that creates a void within, and makes him feel empty and hungry so long as that gap is not filled up. But there comes a time when a prize, lovely or glittering, presents itself, that converts into a barren and sandy waste this whole everyday land of milk and honey; a sight has met the eye, a chord is struck, a sense is awakened, a new and fatal discovery is made; the powers of fascination have thrown their spells over him, and a soul that was free a minute ago is captive and enthralled. No human mind has an immunity from the danger of such attacks; every one is exposed to the chance of some powerful fascination, whatever be the texture of his mind, coarse or refined, that of an angel or that of a brute,—he is exposed to it as being a man.

And so Roberts became obsessed. "He will have this new absorbing prize or nothing"; and he set in train the events, spread over four years, that brought him to his sorry end in the mortuary of Charing Cross Hospital.

The *Times* argued that this obsession, so tirelessly pursued to its violent climax, suggested insanity:

> It is the unnatural strength of what is purely mental *disease* which produces that tremendous exhibition of power of a certain

kind. . . . The madman is stronger than the sane man. It is when such fascination, whether designed or not in the quarter from which it comes, has worked upon a man and endowed some object with an absolute supremacy, and when the man's mind is completely carried off and drained into the excrescence of one swollen passion, that the greatest degree of mere strength is arrived at. He can then do anything he likes; nothing deters him, and nothing softens him; he is beyond hesitation and faltering.

Differ though it did with its venerable contemporary on other vexed issues in the case, the *Daily Telegraph* saw eye-to-eye with it on this one:

Yes; William John Roberts must have been decidedly mad, as mad as any number of March hares. Who but a lunatic would have accosted a gentleman who had never seen him before in his life— never been to his chambers—never been on his staircase—never knocked at his door—accosted him in the open street at high noon, and begged him to take a little walk with him into Northumberland Street, for the purpose of borrowing fifty thousand pounds! Who but an insane person would have given the name of Gray to his new-found acquaintance, forgetting that any man in his senses, when he went to an office with an entire stranger, and finding a number of names on the door-post, would naturally look to see if the name given to him was among them? Who but a raving maniac, intent even on murder, would slay a man at twelve o'clock in the day in his own rooms? How did Roberts propose to dispose of Major Murray's corpse? Was it to lie and rot there in Northumberland-street, amidst the wine bottles, the waste papers, and the articles of vertù? Did he intend to cut him up, as Greenacre cut up Mrs. Brown, or cram the mangled pieces into a carpet bag, and drop them over Waterloo Bridge?* Roberts must have been cunning indeed. All the cunning, all the clearheadedness necessary to the successful prosecution of his calling must have deserted him. He must have lusted after Miss Moody, and, in his rage at not being able to possess her, determined to have the blood of Murray. He must have been labouring under an erotic rabies.

*The writer was alluding to two classic murder cases, the Greenacre affair in 1836–37, in the course of which the murderer distributed his victim's remains at several London sites, and the Waterloo Bridge mystery in 1857, involving a dismembered body that was never identified.

Roberts was not the only protagonist whose balance of mind the press questioned. "Are the delinquents in each case madmen?" demanded the *Morning Post* on the Tuesday after the two sensations first appeared in its columns. "It seems almost conceivable," it said, "that any man of ordinary acuteness (such as the Baron de Vidil is at the least) should have resorted to such an extraordinarily clumsy method of committing so horrible a crime, supposing the act to have proceeded from previous deliberation."

> Had he succeeded [said the *Morning Chronicle*], he would have put everybody on his track; for highway robbery and murder are by no means common events in our Surrey lanes, and suspicion would surely have fastened itself on the Baron, who had been in his victim's company all the afternoon. Such precautions as he took—utterly frivolous as they were—would tend to throw a shade of doubt over the whole narrative, and to be explicable only on the ground of a quick personal quarrel, or of sudden insanity.

The *Morning Post* reported that "a royal personage who saw the baron and his son immediately before the murder was attempted, was much impressed with the remarkable demeanour of the former, who complained, in the course of his visit to the royal duke, of severe pains in his head, and announced that he came to present his son, who, nevertheless, as he asserted, was becoming a monomaniac. So light and airy a fabric of extenuation," the writer admitted, "may, we apprehend, be readily blown down, although it is but just to take into consideration the estimate formed by an intelligent and dispassionate witness of the conduct of the father before the commission of the act."

The question of young Alfred's sanity had been briefly hinted at in reports of the Bow Street hearing and was raised again, more explicitly but still inconclusively, at the Old Bailey. When the verdict was in, the *Morning Advertiser*, availing itself of the same freedom of innuendo that Serjeant Ballantine had claimed, deduced from its own refusal to believe that the son was "a person of healthy mind" a corollary point:

> Nor is it improbable that his mental deficiency, to whatever extent it exists, may have been inherited from his father. Indeed, if we admit the theory that the *Baron* assaulted his son with intent to murder him, the fact that he adopted such a course, under such circumstances, and in a place in which, however lonely it might be, it was impossible to be secure that there was no one looking

on, looks not unlike the act of a lunatic. It is therefore possible—
we cannot pretend to say more—that, had the son submitted
himself to cross-examination, facts might have been elicited which
would have put a different face upon the assault, by showing that
it was not the result of premeditated design.

Whether or not it was a symptom of insanity, the peculiar brutality of the attacks in both Northumberland Street and the Twickenham lane particularly troubled the editorial writers, their tone
and choice of analogies implying that, though violent crime was no
stranger to English soil, it should somehow be conducted with the
modicum of civility that firearms, or, even better, poison discreetly
administered, allowed. If ferocity sometimes did get the better of
good judgment, it normally occurred in territories that, though physically adjacent to the heart of British civilization, were inhabited by
savages. As the *Morning Chronicle* put it,

> It is in no degraded purlieu, no haunt of pugilists and blacklegs,
> no slum of Bermondsey, or cellar of Houndsditch, overflowing
> with fleas and Jews, that the deadly encounter took place, but in
> the chambers of a gentleman . . . Surely nothing more barbarous
> ever occurred in the blackest epochs of our social history. In the
> broad light of day, in the very centre of a civilised metropolis,
> with immense multitudes pouring down contiguous thorough-
> fares, on the banks of the Thames, and with an utter recklessness
> of consequences, a major in the British army and a money-lender
> engage in a contest, such as travellers have rarely witnessed
> among the most ferocious inhabitants of the earth or in the most
> desolate countries. It is not a mere duel, such as American des-
> peradoes have fought with revolvers or bowie knives in pitch dark
> barns; it is not a trial of strength and skill, such as used to be
> made by two half-savage knights, armed with daggers and battle
> axes; it is not even the bloody struggle of two fairly-matched
> Cherokees; it must have been something more dire and vengeful
> than any of these, on one side or the other, and the spring of an
> infuriated beast upon an unsuspecting victim. . . . Talk of the
> Italian knife! What is it to an English pair of tongs? When was the
> victim of Venetian assassination ever discovered huddled shape-
> lessly into a corner with his skull almost falling to pieces, his face
> smashed into a red pulp, and his jaw bone driven into his mouth?
> They formerly punished a poisoner in France by slowly pounding
> his head with an iron mace, but the ferocity which inflicted the

wounds on Mr. Roberts seems to have been beyond that of the club-bearers in Dahomey.

The savagery of Baron de Vidil's own attack did not escape comment; the assault, said the *Morning Herald*, was "marked by such brutal ferocity that it can hardly be credited as occurring between savages of hostile tribes." But this was not the aspect of the man and his deed that most concerned the press. Instead, his seemingly careful planning and deviousness proclaimed his nationality. "To kill a human being," observed one paper, "would seem a thing easy enough to do, if you once screw your courage to the sticking-place; but the Baron soared above the level of Islington butcher-boys. He was a Frenchman, and among our imaginative neighbours crime almost ceases to be crime, if it is perpetrated with proper melodramatic accompaniments. . . . Surely none but a Frenchman, brought up in the school of Sue and Dumas, would have gone such a roundabout way to commit a crime."

That the baron was French undoubtedly biased the London press against him, although admittedly its prejudice against a supposed British veteran of the Crimea was much more blatant until, at length, he was vindicated as a stout warrior who somehow managed to triumph over crushing odds in his moment of peril. It was a mild count—indeed, the only count—in the baron's favor that he rejected the option he had of remaining in France to be tried under the presumably more lenient French system of justice. As the Paris correspondent of the *Daily News* suggested when early rumor had it that the son was dead, there might be some advantage in this, "because, assuming the facts as stated, he would be hanged to a certainty by a British jury, whereas there is no knowing whether a French one, palpitating under the excitement caused by an eloquent speech, might not consider the great need in which the culprit stood of his son-in-law's property, as constituting 'extenuating circumstances.'" Instead, he accepted extradition firm in the conviction that he would receive a fair trial and even waived his right, as a foreigner, to be tried by a jury composed half of British citizens and half of foreigners. As one paper said, he thereby placed English jurisprudence itself on trial: "The eyes of France and of foreign countries in general are upon us here." And the result of the Old Bailey trial satisfied the press not only because the verdict was in accordance with the facts as presented but also because it proved to the world that English justice, put to a severe strain by the unusual circumstances of the case, could and did work.

This was one consolation the outcome of the Vidil case provided to editorialists whose confidence in the nation's social soundness was shaken, for various reasons, by both it and the Northumberland Street affair. The presence of crime was a nagging social issue in mid-Victorian times that was made all the more insistent by the high visibility the press afforded to felonies of all kinds. Because the statistical method of describing and quantifying social phenomena was as yet in its infancy, no reliable figures on the prevalence of crime were to be had, but in some quarters the feeling was that its incidence was steadily increasing.

The events in the summer of 1861 intensified the concern that was generally felt on this score by observers of the nation's well-being. As a writer on "Manners and Morals, As Affected by Civilization" put it in the September issue of *Fraser's Magazine*,

> Just as the appalling procession of last year's criminal train was fading from remembrance, and the great Road tragedy itself sinking to comparative oblivion, there comes a strong stimulant in the shape of the *Fearful Encounter in Northumberland-street*, with the dark revelations of its gloomy sequel; and the barbarous attack of a father upon a son, in the very centre of civilisation, and in the open light of day. Society, which appears to be so light and superficial, and on which the surface bubbles are so numerous and bright, is every now and then startled from its placidity by some unusual testimony to the deadly strength of the rapid currents which whirl and eddy beneath. That the fierce passions of men are not tamed by the progress of civilization is evidenced by the prevalence of deadly outbreaks, such as a few months ago wrung from the *Times* an appeal to the rulers of the people, to "diminish crime by terror, if they could not do so by discipline;" and further to complain, "that in the middle of the nineteenth century, when education has been so long at work, and when civilization is considered so triumphant, it was called upon to record and discuss such numerous and shocking examples of crime."

The *Times's* dark recommendation that the state use "terror" where "discipline" failed undoubtedly alluded to the criminal propensities of the lower classes as they fought and sometimes killed one another in the Bermondsey slums and Houndsditch cellars. The prevalence of crime in the swelling city slums and the miserable hovels of the rural poor was a perennial source of worry to guardians of the national morality, who generally prescribed two preventives in addition to the administration of soporific religion: a smattering of education (though in some quarters teaching the poor to write was viewed as an open invitation to them to become a race of forgers) and making it harder for them to get drunk. But now it seemed increasingly evident that vice and crime had become, as it were, upwardly mobile, occurring where they had seldom been seen before, in the very precincts of middle-class life. To be sure, this impression may have been partially illusory. The thriving newspaper press was affording unprecedented publicity to felonies, nonviolent (such as fraud and embezzlement) and violent alike, but not on a uniform basis: it skewed the news. As the *Saturday Review* (like the *Spectator*, not a newspaper but a weekly literary journal) remarked:

> Newspaper reports tell us more about the middle classes because the middle class is the most numerous, and is that in which violations of the social laws most naturally come into the publicity of Courts of Justice. The profligacy of high life and the brutality of low life more frequently escape public attention, because, in the one case, concealment is a matter of interest, and in the other there is no call from public opinion to parade, or even to correct, private wrong. An intrigue in Belgravia and a brutal assault in Whitechapel escape that publicity which is sure to attend vice in Bloomsbury [then the prototype of a quiet middle-class London neighborhood]. All that we can at present say about vice in Bloomsbury is, that we happen to hear more about it than about vice elsewhere; but it would be premature to conclude that the late homicide in Northumberland-street . . . [is] to be taken as a sign of the times, or evidence of the state of commonplace English life.

The *Standard* made another point: in an undeterminable number of instances, justice was blind or looked the other way. In lack of an efficient and impartial system by which "murder, violence, arson, burglary, and all the worst offences" might be detected and the perpetrators brought to trial, "cases of the kind occur even in our well-regulated society which are muffled up to spare the feelings of sentimental or scrupulous relations and friends."

Whatever the number of grave crimes in middle- and upper-class life that went unpublicized, those involving Major Murray and Baron de Vidil were decidedly not among them. And it was the social milieu in which each crime occurred that, along with the psychological mysteries involved, fascinated the readership of the press.

Men of like passions, and, more than this, men of the same social standing and pretensions as ourselves [said the *Saturday Review*], are the actors and victims in these dreadful tragedies. Some of us may have known personally either Mr. Roberts, or Major Murray, or the MM. de Vidil. There is no reason why we should not have dined in their company but the other day. Murder is brought very home and close, not only to greater numbers of people, but to different people from those before whom it presented itself in former times and under different social conditions. It seems to be almost a thing of ourselves when it walks about unabashed at mid-day in Northumberland-street, and scarcely condescends to hide in the populous publicity of Twickenham lanes.

The shock which the story of Roberts's passionate pursuit of Mrs. Murray administered to those who avidly read her testimony, said the same paper in a later issue, resided largely in his very commonplaceness, his utter recognizability:

Mr. Roberts' life was not perhaps the most reputable form of business life; still it was, externally, that of the staid, regular, moral man of middle-class life and middle age. His was the type of respectability and propriety—the type of the man who goes to business every day, has his office and his home, with wife and family, and all that is decorous about him. It may be that his particular kind of business would not always bear a very close scrutiny. He dealt in money, and he occasionally found means for other people to do a little business under fictitious names; and his line of business was that of agency and commission, and brokerage and percentage. But what of all this? There are thousands of wives who cannot tell what exact line of business their husbands pursue. All that they know is that they go down to "the office" and come home to dinner, by the train or in the omnibus. . . . And if you follow Mr. Roberts to his decorous home, there is nothing to stimulate suspicion. He goes to the Crystal Palace with his wife and son, or he has his little Sunday dissipation at Spurgeon's, all in the staid, sober, domestic, respectable way. . . . But behind, there is a burning, maddening passion in this decent, respectable gentleman of more than middle age, consuming and eating out not only his soul, but even destroying every prudential consideration. . . . It was the passion of a wild beast rather than of a man—only the wild beast was, after all, a prosaic London bill-discounter.

The *Saturday Review*'s analysis accurately suggests the uneasiness mid-Victorian society felt over the recurrent indications, supplied especially by criminal deeds, that beneath their feet were dangerous unplumbed depths, uncontrollable forces that constantly threatened the peace and stability of their social system. In a direct, stark confrontation, middle-class respectability evidently was no match for remorseless passion, even when harbored within the bosom of an outwardly staid London businessman.

At the outset of the furor the *Daily Telegraph* assumed the mantle of the "speculative philosopher" which it would wear for the duration of the two cases. It was sure there was an explanation for "the extraordinary concurrence in deeds of crime or of bloodshed—the appetite, so to speak, of Nature to 'sup full of horrors'"—but was less sure what caused it:

> It were idle to attempt to account for such a concurrence . . . by throwing it all to the account of the "law of averages." What is such a law, what such a doctrine, but a feeble endeavour to formulate into knowledge that which we do not know? . . . We may calculate on the appearance of a comet, but who can predict a run upon forgery, upon robbery, upon murder by the poison phial or assassination by the knife? That one such crime may beget another, that continual brooding over the history of a dreadful deed may incite in certain morbid conditions of mind a disposition to imitate it, we can well understand; but how is it when we find concurrent crimes committed in localities far apart, under circumstances directly similar as to character, but with motives diametrically opposite, and by persons who by scarcely a human possibility could have had any knowledge of each other? Is there at times some moral malaria in the air, travelling, like cholera, with unerring pace, tainting now some chosen victim and sparing his neighbour?

The question may have been intended rhetorically, but the *Illustrated Times* (10 August) had a scientific answer:

> That some unusual endemic excitement has been at work, directing weak, debauched, and diseased minds into a homicidal course, must be apparent to every newspaper-reader. May not the electrical condition of the atmosphere exercise some hidden power in this way over the human brain? A correspondent of the *Standard*, Dr. J. Q. Rumball, a well-known lecturer on science,

points out electrical causes as the origin of the potato disorder. It is a fact that lately the finest mechanisms of clockwork, notably those at the Observatory at Greenwich, have been going wrong, without visible internal derangement or imperfection, and this has been attributed to an abnormal condition of atmospheric electricity. It is surely not a wildly-hazardous theory to suppose that a similar agency acting upon that most susceptible and complex of galvanic machines, the human brain, may have some tendency, if not to the actual increase of crime, of lessening the healthy power which restrains its committal or of aggravating the phrenal disease which but for such influence might have been subdued, or at least retarded.

The hypothesis was typical of more than a little Victorian science—half wrong and half right. Although the connection between rotten potatoes, erratic timepieces at Greenwich, and a dreadfully battered moneylender in Northumberland Street required a leap of logic as perilous as Blondin's performance on the high wire, the idea that the brain is "that most susceptible and complex of galvanic machines," a marvel of electrochemical circuitry, lies at the heart of modern neurological thought.

Like the *Daily Telegraph*, the *Saturday Review* worried about the likelihood of what we today call "copycat" crimes:

The newspaper intelligence in everybody's hands and mouth invests murder with another kind of familiarity. It is not therefore only the deep dye of these crimes, but the publicity of the details, which now-a-days is so important. Public thought must be influenced in ways and directions of which we can hardly understand the importance, by murders every little detail of which is known to and familiarly canvassed by millions. Fathers, we dare say, have murdered their sons for their inheritance in the ages since Agamemnon was a brave man, and undoubtedly a scuffle for life has been fought out ere now in a solitary room, to the full as deadly as that which took place in Northumberland-street last week; but the sacred poet of the penny papers did not sing these things. For one person who talked over the bloody murder of the baron two centuries ago, and under other conditions of European life, perhaps a hundred thousand canvass a similar deed now. When everybody dwells upon it—makes it the subject of his daily conversation and his nightly dreams—we are presented with a state of things which is well worthy of consideration.

Whether or not the minutely described modus operandi of each antagonist tempted impressionable middle-class minds to consider similar deeds, the publicity each crime received must have had a marked, though perhaps subtle, effect on private morality. The *Saturday Review* made this point in a later editorial on the Northumberland Street case:

> It is the natural tendency of familiarity with great crime to produce a sort of tenderness and sympathy with it, when its perpetrators and victims are the sort of people we meet with every day. . . . We deprecate the notion of young or middle-aged gentlemen getting to think that it is not a very outrageous, or a very horrid and uncommon thing, for a decent married man to make love on the sly, and with the assistance of his money influences, to his neighbour's wife or his neighbour's mistress, and to use his offices in the city for carrying on a vulgar intrigue of this description.

The journalistic soul-searching on behalf of the nation at large continued through most of August. The "moral malaria" of which the *Daily Telegraph* had spoken—the *Morning Chronicle* called it an "ulcerous social wound" a few days later—was taken to be endemic in present-day life. The relations between father and son, even the small glimpse that the trial evidence allowed, said the *Morning Herald*, "would go far—if supposed to imply a practice of a general kind—to explain much of the social disorganisation of which all classes in society are now complaining. . . . Are these the relations of father and son—in married life too—to which we are coming? Is this an essential part of modern society to which our improvements are bringing us? Are such men—'the observed of all observers,' the guests of Emperors, the friends of abdicated monarchies, the ruling spirits of fashionable clubs—to take rank amongst us as the best products we have to offer of our advancing civilisation?" A day later, the *Standard* took up the prophetic cry:

> Society may possibly go on even in very high states of civilisation, under almost any conditions of hidden or overt attack on life or property; but if these conditions should ever come to the point which, it would seem, was reached for brief periods in some of the social circles of Imperial and medieval Rome, when what is happily now the exception in human nature proved the rule, we should want no agency of fiends to turn the fairest of human lots into a hell. The contagion of crime is catching and reactive. Happily the devices that may be very profitable in their initiation are

felt less agreeable when they come back "to plague the inventor." It is a law of life that crime will be eaten up by crime, and perhaps as society goes on our best security is that it would be a very foolish colony of crime that would not invent virtue for its own sake.

The *Morning Chronicle* had earlier invoked a supposed parallel in history that had extra timeliness thanks to Vidil's association with the exiled Orleanist family: "A similar series of crimes preceded, and to wise men seemed to prognosticate, the fall of Louis Philippe. Are we to expect a national catastrophe in England, or are we not rather to look upon the deeds we have been enumerating as mere excrescences, not the fungus that springs on the fermenting dung-hill, but the weed that, despite all the gardener's care, will shoot up to mar the beauty of his borders?" The writer's conclusion was more sanguine than those of some of his colleagues: "We believe the middle classes to be free from the demoralisation, of which the frauds and the violence recounted above are symptoms. We have all of us shortcomings enough to answer for, but we believe the core of society to be sound enough. Were it not so, we should, indeed, tremble for our country. . . . We cannot . . . charge society with a crime [such as Vidil's] which is manifestly an exception. It would be just as rational to condemn a whole vintage because at your last whitebait dinner the waiter brought you a 'corked' bottle of claret."

The *Spectator*, too, rejecting the opinion it attributed to the public, that the assaults were "a disgrace to the nineteenth century," denied that they had anything to do with the true spirit of the age:

The specialty of the nineteenth century is material progress, which can no more affect the average of ordinary murders than it can change the laws of light, or make a bad smell otherwise than annoying. The passions, which are the causes of murder, are not abolished by new inventions. Nobody has discovered a machine for extinguishing hate, or an instrument for extracting revenge, or even a powder to diminish the force of jealousy, and those are the true sources of the majority of murders. The great remaining cause, the desire for wealth, is positively increased by a civilization which permits money to purchase everything except a clean conscience and a cool breeze. . . . There *are* murders, no doubt, which, if frequently repeated, would indicate that our civilization was unsound, that the national heart amidst its prosperity, or because of its prosperity, was becoming exceptionally depraved.

The story would be different if, for example, there was a widespread resort to poisoning as in medieval Italian cities, or if, as was alleged (but the *Spectator* took leave to doubt), infanticide was widely practiced in the north of England for the sake of collecting, and misspending, burial insurance. The Vidil and Murray cases, it continued, were "crimes committed from ordinary motives, and by the most brutal and stupid of means." How could civilization prevent a deed like Vidil's? "All the civilization conceivable will not diminish the power of any man who chooses to hit down any other with a riding-whip." As for the Northumberland Street confrontation, "that two men, mad with jealousy, should quarrel for some letters, proceed to blows, and then to a death-grapple, that surely is not an incident condemning the nineteenth century."

"The real reason to be learnt from these occurrences," the writer concluded, "is not to be taught by vain rhetoric about the hollowness of a civilization which has no influence in the matter. They furnish an additional illustration of the oft-repeated argument, that our laws fail altogether to repress brutality. They are, indeed, absurdly lenient. There is a keen horror of murder among Englishmen, but there is a great tolerance for the brutality which so often ends in the hated crime." It was to brutal street assaults, for example, which reveal that "in the midst of our civilization there is an entire class neither softened nor placed under needful discipline," that would-be reformers should direct their energies, by pushing for stiffened penalties.* And so the *Spectator* lined itself up four-square with the *Times*:

> Terror is a bad instrument of government, but there are some impulses, and the impulse to murder is one of them, which can be repressed only by another emotion acting as quickly and powerfully as themselves. The only such emotion human beings have at their disposal is terror, and it is by an unswerving but just severity, and not by common-places about progress, that scenes like those of the past week are to be made less frequent.

A week later, the *News of the World*, rejecting the *Spectator's* draconian proposal but sharing its opinion of the unredeemed soul of man, waxed less alarmist and more philosophical:

---

*A year later, in the autumn of 1862, street assaults took a new and frightening turn as robbers garrotted (throttled) their victims—a particularly vicious form of mugging.

There has been some very silly would-be philosophising upon these occurrences amongst people who accustom themselves to praise of "the nineteenth century;" and because these transactions seem to militate against the views of progress which are so industriously circulated by shallow thinkers who have not looked for causes, a silly outcry is raised that the life of Englishmen is disgraced by such attacks. All this is very stupid. The world wags on, and every now and then there is a little progress to be noted; but it is too much to expect that murder is to cease simply because commerce increases, and books and mechanics' institutes flourish. The human passions are passions still, and they are just as likely to be stirred by commercial motives as speedily as by others. It is equally false to glorify our age, as to pronounce its disgrace. Its glory is not to be found merely in abstinence from murder, or its disgrace because Baron de Vidil attacks his son. It is only very superficial thinkers who arrive at such conclusions. The truth, if we had the courage to state it, is that the age in which we live has its faults as well as its advantages, and one of these is that, bearing in mind the increase of population and the increase of the motives of crime, we have also to deal with the fair average of criminals. Nor have we any right to expect any other than a gradual increase of crime. We may multiply policemen, build gaols, and increase punishments; but we cannot prevent men becoming possessed of the love of money, and when drawn into a corner, trying to conceal their shame by the death or silence of another. It is because we overrate the tendencies of the age in which we live, that we display this over-sensitiveness as to a particular crime. But this very feeling of sensitiveness is a valuable safeguard against the criminal, because it converts us all into extra-detectives. And it is not only in paid supervision of criminals that we must trust. We can only expect to destroy the motives to crime when we succeed in surrounding that portion of society whose tendencies are towards crime, with such surveillance from the eyes of the community as to render crime impossible, or, at all events, unprofitable. Crime will cease to be profitable when society is willing to surrender its share in the profits of criminals. There could not be thieves if there were not receivers; and perhaps there would not be homicides if there were not legacies and debts. But it is not always the murderer or the burglar who is influenced by a greedy motive. There is a sympathy with criminals largely shared by many respectable members of society, or who

seem to be such, and it seldom happens that a great crime bene-
fits only the criminal. . . . Our Cains who kill for gold can never
be sure for whom they work. Of course the merely malicious man
will continue to kill and destroy, but generally speaking, in such
attempts to compass their designs there is enough of passion and
the heat of blood to reduce the crime to manslaughter in the language of the law. When every homicide comes to be fully examined, it will be found that there is no reason to believe that we are
more cruel or more passionate than our forefathers. But an analysis of our crimes will show us that ignorance is not the only parent of the court calendar, and that the removal of ignorance will
not relieve us from the stroke of the manslayer. Even when we
admit so much it does not follow we should weep over a fallen
country, but it ought to prevent us unduly glorifying our age.
None of the crimes committed lately disclose any increase in the
intelligence of criminals; no new mode of death has been discovered; no new passion has been called into existence. We have just
to deal with ordinary passions and motives as we have had to do
for centuries past. Our agencies for detection are generally successful; we may not hope that detection will always lead to pre-
vention. Human nature is just as bad in some people as it always
was; what improvement there is is found in the numbers represented by, and is absorbed in, the increase of population.

To most readers, this philosophical reassurance perhaps carried
less weight than the more immediate one the *Saturday Review* adopted.
The career and fate of Roberts, it said, should not delude us that un-
counted prospective murderers lurked wherever a great city carried
on its lawful everyday activities: "His life was, in its outside shape
and form, the life of thousands of men of business; but our middle
classes are not to be judged by Mr. Roberts. The case only shows that
great tragic deeds and passions—the passions of Macbeths, and
Othellos, and Cencis—may be about us and around us in omnibuses
and penny steamboats; but this is no reason why we should suspect
everybody we meet in omnibuses or penny steamboats."

CHAPTER FOUR

From Fact to Fiction

From the beginning, the press dramatized the twin sensations that had fallen into its lap in the way it felt would best describe their fabulous quality. Each, it proclaimed, was a case of life imitating—indeed, outdoing—art. "Now," said the *Sunday Times* a fortnight after the disturbance in Northumberland Street, "let a powerful writer of fiction take those facts, and work them up into an elaborate story, retaining the situation and the time of the event, and not exaggerating its manner in the slightest possible degree; and the critics of the country will all denounce his work for the monstrous improbabilities on which he had relied for effect. Yet about the reality of the case there unfortunately is no room whatever for doubt. The fiction would be condemned as an absurdity; the fact stands exempt from dispute or question of any kind!" A week earlier, the *Saturday Review* had provided a similar estimate of the Vidil case from the literary point of view, recording, as it did so, an early rumor that until then evidently had not surfaced in print:

> All the elements of romance familiar to the readers of the circulating library concur in "the Twickenham tragedy;" and there actually seems to be evidence for what almost everybody, when it was only the talk of London, set down as the hallucination of some half-witted youth who had, perhaps, under the influence of mental disease, attempted to embody in fact a study of Mr. Reynolds' full-bodied novels. French barons, the personal friends of Royal exiles, who marry English wives, and get entangled in pecuniary difficulties with their own sons, and attempt assassinations in shady lanes in the pastoral suburbs of London, are usually

thought to be mythical characters. But much of what is alleged of the Baron de Vidil's curious career remains without contradiction; and there is very clear and distinct evidence of at least an actual assault of a severe character.

"As to the Northumberland-street assault," the writer continued,

> it seems to concentrate and exhaust all the accredited common-places of the romantic drama. Everything is of that thrilling interest which has hitherto been only possible at the minor theatres, or in tales published in weekly penny numbers. It is only in the *Mysteries of the Court of London* [by G.W.M. Reynolds, mentioned above], or in the pages of M. Dumas, that bill-brokers live in apartments furnished and decorated with regal wealth, and sumptuous alike in splendour and an accumulation of treasured dust. We have occasionally heard of, but no human being ever met, that conventional hero of the *feuilleton*, who never suffered the solitude of his mysterious rooms overhanging the river to be broken by the intrusion of servants.

If one read of such persons and events in fiction, one willingly suspended disbelief; now disbelief must be suspended again as the amazing "true" tales unfolded.

The very day the stories broke, two papers laced their coverage and comment on the Vidil affair with literary allusions. The *Morning Chronicle* began its report by saying, "The story about to be told is unparalleled in the annals of crime, in the romance of private life, or in those stories of domestic tragedy familiar to every English fireside." The *Daily Telegraph* devoted an entire paragraph in its leader to elaborating on the same idea:

> What a strange and terrible story is that which a contemporary [the *Morning Post*] has furnished us with, and which appears in our columns this day! As we peruse its startling details we seem to be reading a chapter from Frédéric Soulié or from Paul Féval, rather than the narrative of an occurrence which took place on the outskirts of this metropolis, and which is doubtless destined ere long to claim a page in Old Bailey annals. Indeed, the tale may be said to pass far beyond the bounds of fictitious romance, and to stand apart by itself, like the Praslin tragedy of modern times,*

---

*In 1847, in one of the series of crimes that, according to the *Morning Chronicle*, had portended the fall of Louis Philippe, the Duchesse de Praslin was found stabbed to death in her bed.

or the Borgia poisonings of the middle ages. What novelist of the present day, even though as fond of the morbid as Poe, or of the marvellous as Dumas, would take for his theme the attempt of a father upon his son's life, the son being a grown man, and the cause of the outrage against him the desire to obtain an inheritance to which he was entitled? What writer of fiction, moreover, would place the scene of this attempted murder just beyond the suburbs of London, in a rural lane, along which labourers were passing at the moment of the occurrence, the time being the very middle of a summer day? [Actually, the assault took place about seven in the evening.] We should reject as improbable, almost as absurd, such a melodramatic incident, and close the book with a yawn or fling it from us in disgust. If, too, the author had introduced the father to us as a nobleman, moving in the very first society, member of a fashionable club, connected by marriage with an ancient and wealthy family—nay, received as a cherished guest by Royalty itself; if he had added these details to his picture, we should have looked upon the work as the product of a vulgar intellect, intended only for the gratification of minds as morbid and as diseased as his own. Yet this strange story is given to us as the record of an actual event, with a circumstantial minuteness and an evidence of authenticity which go far to rob it of its improbability, and to leave incredulity without a basis to rest upon.

The following Monday (15 July), the *Morning Chronicle* recalled that three columns in its Saturday edition "were filled with the narration of two domestic tragedies which we might almost fancy to have been drawn from the stimulating pages of a French romance, so much do they exceed the inventive powers of the humble penny-a-liner." Describing the attack in "the pretty shady lanes between Claremont and Twickenham" ("the groves of Twickenham, where Pope, and in our day Tennyson, dwelt," another paper reminded its readers a week later), the *Morning Chronicle* stressed that the baron "was a Frenchman, and among our imaginative neighbours crime almost ceases to be crime, if it is perpetrated with proper melodramatic accompaniments. . . . Surely none but a Frenchman, brought up in the school of Sue and Dumas, would have gone such a roundabout way to commit a crime." Three papers (the *Times*, 16 July; the *Morning Chronicle*, 20 July; and the *Morning Post*, 26 July) compared the furnishings of Roberts's rooms to the interior decor of a French romance, and two others (the *Examiner*, 27 July; and the *Saturday Review*, 3 August)

revived the earlier likening of the stories themselves to those of
Dumas—except that, they said, these real-life events strained credulity even farther than he did. This concurrence of quickly plati-
tudinous analogies offers fairly impressive evidence of the way the
English literary imagination in respect to popular "romantic" narratives was dominated at this period by Dumas.

The *Times*'s editorial on the dénouement of the Northumberland
Street mystery was wholly structured on the notion of a certain variety of "coarse romance" (not necessarily French, though perhaps this
was implied) which Roberts's obsession with Mrs. Murray represented. Here, what was written as a journalistic analysis of a real-life
situation verged on literary criticism with psychological under-
pinnings:

> In this case we have the romance of uncontrolled passion. Some
> people as soon as they hear that word expect something great, re-
> fined, and sublime; but this is not at all necessary for romance,
> and in Mr. Roberts' case every characteristic of this kind is con-
> spicuously absent. It is from beginning to end the most coarse,
> degrading, and vulgar affair that can be conceived. All that is nec-
> essary for romance is that there should be *strength* in it. It is like
> the case of language. Strong language need not be choice or ele-
> gant,—indeed, some talkers think it cannot be.

Reviewing the several actions that manifested Roberts's infatuation,
the *Times* continued:

> All this is as coarse, disgusting, and brutal as can be imagined;
> yet with the horrible death-struggle in the rooms, and with the
> obstinately taciturn death lastly of Mr. Roberts himself in the hos-
> pital, it is a *romance*. Why? Because at the bottom of the whole lies
> one powerful, absorbing, and uncontrollable passion. Healthy
> motives and healthy moral temperaments do not furnish many
> victims for romance of any kind, high or low.

But Roberts was not sane but insane, and "the madman is stronger
than the sane man"; he possessed "the brutal strength of coarse romance," and when he resolved to pursue his prize who dwelt in
Major Murray's Tottenham retreat, we "have a romance—an exces-
sively low and vulgar one perhaps, but still a romance." Such, the
Times concluded,

> appears to be the explanation of this horrible Northumberland-
> street tragedy. Whatever Mr. Roberts was—and it is plain enough

what he was—he was in a romantic state of mind in the sense which we have been describing; he was under that influence which may overcome the greatest blackguard in the world—the influence of an overwhelming fascination. . . . Mr. Roberts was thus converted . . . into a perfect Colossus of romance, with a will like that of a Titan.

Although the commentators stressed the French-romance angle, their literary allusions ranged from Poe ("We have no Poe amongst us now to penetrate this mystery, and arrive through a dark labyrinth of evidence and deduction at that mental standpoint where all becomes open and clear," said the *Daily Telegraph* as it wound up its coverage of the Vidil case) to the Babes in the Wood, a rather inept comparison, as the *Morning Chronicle* recognized when it invoked it in speaking of the Vidils: "One of them at least [was] not quite so innocent."

In pronouncing their last words on the Northumberland Street affair, one paper after another ended on the note on which they had begun, their assertion that the case belonged more appropriately in the treasury of the literary imagination than the annals of real-life crime. "The curtain has fallen," said the *Morning Chronicle*, "on the conclusion of the last act of this horrid tragedy, and the audience depart with a feeling that however terrific and melodramatic the incidents, substantial justice has been done." "A motive for the crime has certainly been disclosed," the *Morning Post* concluded, "but of so slight a character as scarcely to deserve the name, and such as none but a novelist writing for a penny miscellany would think of representing as the inducement to a cold-blooded and deliberate murder. . . . If this story be true, let no novelist despair: the flimsiest of motives will suffice on which to hang a deed of crime; and if critics should prove captious, let him refer with triumph to the story of the Northumberland-street tragedy."

Given the literary examples to which the newspapers alluded in their search for ready analogues, it was only to be expected that the writers' prose might sometimes reflect their personal familiarity with such literature. "We are hardly surprised at the vivid language of the gentlemen of the press," commented the *Saturday Review*. "With so large a canvas, and a subject so stimulating, even a sober painter might be pardoned for the free hand with which the blood was dashed about, and with which the accessories of the lawyer-discounter's rooms are drawn, or rather coloured, by the Fuselis of the penny papers"— an obvious, and unkind, reference to the three penny *Times*'s notorious exercise in scene painting. But narrative style was infected too. Witness the *Morning Herald's* intimate depiction of Major Murray's finest moment:

> The flow of blood [caused by Roberts's second bullet] brought back consciousness to the bewildered Murray, and a consciousness of his position has furnished to the world an instance of self-possession and cool intrepidity seldom paralleled. It was now the major's turn to dissemble. With the blood bubbling out from his wound and over his face in a torrent, in the very whirl and maze of every conflicting emotion, he made up his mind to pretend he was dead, as the narrative runs. He felt his murderer's warm breath as he stooped to peer into his state, and ascertain whether the foul plot had succeeded. But he compressed his own breathing, stifled every surging passion, drove back every rising fear, and whilst he simulated death externally internally pondered over the chances of life. At length the tide of fortune changed, but the struggle was yet to commence. Roberts retired to a distant part of the room. The major opened his eyes, closed in death to all appearances; seized a pair of tongs that were near at hand, rushed and struck at his antagonist with all his might. The blow missed its object, but despair had re-invigorated his sinking frame. He grappled with and threw the murderer. He changed his weapon. Seizing whatever was at hand and convenient, he struck wildly and heavily at his assailant. At last the conflict turned in his favour.

"All these incidents," said the *Daily Telegraph*, "read marvellously like a column of graphic description from an American newspaper." But the London paper, whose own reporters and editorial writers were no novices at graphic description, did not have to reach across the Atlantic for a journalistic or literary scapegoat. Such crudely vivid prose was endemic in the penny dreadfuls and shilling shockers that sold by the millions of copies in mid-Victorian England.

Of all those who commented on the Northumberland Street tragedy, it was Thackeray, a former journalist himself, who wrote the definitive appreciation of it from the novelist's point of view. In the September issue of the *Cornhill Magazine*, which he edited, he published one of his ongoing series of Roundabout Papers, titled "On Two Roundabout Papers Which I Intended to Write."

> The first was that Northumberland Street encounter, which all the papers have narrated. Have any novelists of our days a scene and catastrophe more strange and terrible than this which occurs at noonday within a few yards of the greatest thoroughfare in

Europe? At the theatres they have a new name for their melodramatic pieces, and call them "Sensation Dramas." What a sen-
sation drama this is! What have people been flocking to see at the
Adelphi Theatre for the last hundred and fifty nights? A woman
pitched overboard out of a boat, and a certain Dan [actually
Miles] taking a tremendous "header," and bringing her to shore?
[This was Boucicault's *The Colleen Bawn*, to be mentioned below.]
Bagatelle! What is this compared to the real life drama, of which a
midday representation takes place just opposite the Adelphi in
Northumberland Street? The brave Dumas, the intrepid Ainsworth, the terrible Eugène Sue, the cold-shudder inspiring
Woman in White, the astounding author of the *Mysteries of the
Court of London*, never invented anything more tremendous than
this. It might have happened to you and me. We want to borrow a
little money. We are directed to an agent. We propose a pecuniary
transaction at a short date. He goes into the next room, as we
fancy, to get the bank-notes, and returns with "two very pretty,
delicate little ivory-handed pistols," and blows a portion of our
heads off. After this, what is the use of being squeamish about
the probabilities and possibilities in the writing of fiction? Years
ago I remember making merry over a play of Dumas, called *Kean*,
in which the Coal-Hole Tavern was represented on the Thames,
with a fleet of pirate ships anchored alongside. Pirate ships? Why
not? What a cavern of terror was this in Northumberland Street,
with its splendid furniture covered with dust, its empty bottles,
in the midst of which sits a grim "agent," amusing himself by firing pistols, aiming at the unconscious mantelpiece, or at the
heads of his customers? After this, what is not possible? It is possible Hungerford Market is mined, and will explode some day.
Mind how you go for a penny ice unawares. "Pray, step this way,"
says a quiet person at the door. You enter—into a back room:—a
quiet room; rather a dark room. "Pray, take your place in a chair."
And she goes to fetch the penny ice. *Malheureux!* The chair sinks
down with you—sinks, and sinks, and sinks—a large wet flannel
suddenly envelops your face and throttles you. Need we say any
more? After Northumberland Street, what is improbable? Surely
there is no difficulty in crediting Bluebeard. I withdraw my last
month's opinions about ogres.* Ogres? Why not? I protest I have

---

*In the August issue of the *Cornhill* Thackeray had written a set of playful variations
on the fancy that ogres, far from ceasing to exist, survived throughout middle-class
English society, including even the business world. But they now took commonplace,
respectable forms, nothing like the fearsome ones they assumed in old romance and

seldom contemplated anything more terribly ludicrous than this "agent" in the dingy splendour of his den, surrounded by dusty ormolu and piles of empty bottles, firing pistols for his diversion at the mantelpiece until his clients come in! Is pistol practice so common in Northumberland Street, that it passes without notice in the lodging-houses there?

At this point, Thackeray drifted off into a fit of vapid moralizing:

Is there some Northumberland Street chamber in your heart and mine, friend: close to the every-day street of life; visited by daily friends: visited by people on business; in which affairs are transacted; jokes are uttered; wine is drunk; through which people come and go; wives and children pass; and in which murder sits unseen until the terrible moment when he rises up and kills?

And more to the same depressing effect. Then:

I happened to pass, and looked at the Northumberland Street house the other day. A few loiterers were gazing up at the dingy windows. A plain, ordinary face of a house enough—and in a chamber in it one man suddenly rose up, pistol in hand, to slaughter another. . . . I tell you that the sight of those blank windows in Northumberland Street—through which, as it were, my mind could picture the awful tragedy glimmering behind—set me thinking, "Mr. Street-Preacher, here is a text for one of your pavement sermons. But it is too glum and serious. You eschew dark thoughts; and desire to be cheerful and merry in the main." And, such being the case, you see we must have no Roundabout essay on this subject.

This lapse into sentimentality, the bane of Thackeray's art, and the possible hint of his uneasy sense of guilt lurking in the midst of pleasure do not detract significantly from his enthusiasm over the late proceedings in Northumberland Street. If the two cases, along with their saturation press coverage, may be said in retrospect to have been the first sensations of their kind in the swiftly dawning age of sensation, Thackeray's tribute may be read as symbolic recognition on behalf of the literary profession that the age had come into being.

---

nursery story. To Thackeray, in Northumberland Street the ogre figure momentarily reverted to the full-blooded pattern of undomesticated legend. The preceding reference to the sinking chair is plainly intended to associate the event with a familiar London fable, that of the barber-ogre Sweeney Todd, whose customers were converted into meat pies in the cellar of his Fleet Street shop.

As was said in Chapter One, the appetite for what now came to be called sensation was not new; the hunger seems simply to have been more keen, more conscious, and above all more extensively publicized than it was in the past. To some extent, also, it was redirected. Although real-life supplies of the blood-curdling, the heart-stopping, the hair-raising were not diminished (Blondin, for example, had rivals in various lines of daredevil entertainment), the public appetite for the improbable and perilous found its chief satisfaction in the mimetic art of the theater and the narrative art of the novel.

When Thackeray spoke of the "new name" given to what were customarily called "melodramatic pieces" on the stage, he was pinpointing the route by which the word "sensation" was at that moment entering the general vocabulary. From the beginning of the century onward, melodrama had been among the most popular forms of drama for the sole reason that its stock in trade was crude excitement. This excitement derived mainly from suspense and surprise—disguise plots and their unmasking, sudden reversals of fortune, races against time, unexpected last-minute appearances of long-absent characters, revelation of crucial secrets, and other instant dénouements. Emotionally charged scenes produced by such developments were the histrionic actor's meat and drink. But a comparatively new kind of incident, mechanical rather than dramaturgic, made it possible for playwright and manager to move their product another notch higher in the scale of dramatic effect, intensifying the frisson of the unexpected into that produced by danger and/or rescue from novel physical sources. The mechanical and technical innovations that had enhanced the visual appeal of theatrical performances in the past several decades were readily applied to increasing the verisimilitude of scenes representing such sensational events as fires, storms, floods, and explosions. It became possible to produce physical effects on an unprecedented scale and with unprecedented realism. To the thrill of situation was added the thrill derived from visual action that seemed a transcript of perilous, suspenseful moments in real life.

One of the chief reasons for this advance in staging was the demands placed on the theatrical mechanic and scene designer by the burgeoning of elaborate spectacle, notably in Shakespearean productions in which historical authenticity was much prized—a movement reaching its climax in the 1850s with the lavishly mounted productions of Charles Kean and Samuel Phelps. Now the same skills that had been responsible for heightened realism in Shakespearean and historical drama in general were applied to the humbler artifacts of the popular theater. The invention of the box set made it possible to reproduce actual rooms onstage, with practicable doors by which actors could enter and leave instead of through the wings. The old painted flats were replaced by elaborate and fully furnished interior sets (of courtrooms and restaurants, for example) and built-up exteriors of city scenes, in particular familiar locales in London and provincial cities.

But above all, the new melodrama was distinguished by its "sensation scenes"—at least one per play—which were as obligatory as the Venusberg scene Baron de Vidil's own ballet-loving Jockey Club had required Richard Wagner to write for the first Paris production of *Tannhäuser*, only months before the baron took his son for their disastrous ride. The term had entered the London theatrical vocabulary less than a year before Thackeray used it. It had appeared, for instance, in a notice (*Illustrated London News*, 16 March) of a play by E. T. Smith, *The Savannah*. Dion Boucicault claimed to have invented it, but whether or not this is true, the first sensation drama that was customarily so called was undoubtedly his *The Colleen Bawn*, originally produced in New York (March 1860) at the end of his extended sojourn in the United States. This is probably one reason why *Punch* called "sensations" an imported American product. First performed in London at the Adelphi Theatre in the Strand, only a few blocks from Northumberland Street (not opposite it, as Thackeray said) on 10 September 1860, *The Colleen Bawn* had for its coup de théâtre a scene in which the heroine was pitched into the waters of a lake (represented by waves of blue gauze operated by a score of boys), to be rescued by the hero, Miles-na-Coppaleen, after a death-defying dive. The waves were nothing new on the stage (though perhaps these were more realistic), but the dive was a genuine novelty, and thanks to the scene, the play broke all records for a continuous run (230 performances), was the first West End production to be toured, and was attended by the queen and prince consort on no fewer than three occasions.

Quickly responding to the public demand he had created for athletic feats on the part of the actors or startling mechanical innovations—preferably both—in subsequent seasons Boucicault brought on stage a gratifying, and profitable, variety of actions and effects. In *The Octoroon* (November 1861) a Mississippi steamboat caught fire and the villain was unmasked by the operation of a previously set camera that caught him in the act of murder. In *Arrah-na-Pogue* (Dublin, 1864; London, 1865) the hero scaled the ivied tower of the prison in which he had been confined—the tower sinking through the stage to enhance the illusion of a steep climb—fought the villain at the top and then flung him down to his death. In *The Streets of London* (1864) a raging tenement fire was fought by a real fire engine hauled onstage. In *The Long Strike* (1866) an unattended telegraph instrument tapped out a vital message. In *Flying Scud* (also 1866) the Derby was raced by a field of cut-out horses, and the winner—a real horse—was led onstage. In *After Dark* (1868), which borrowed rather blatantly from Augustin Daly's *Under the Gaslight* (New York, 1867), the hero was tied to the track of the London Underground as a train thundered up. Boucicault of course had numerous imitators, and melodramas with sensation scenes continued to prosper until the time of the First World War.

Boucicault's dramas were the most important contribution the stage made to the developing rage for sensation. But the fashion was reflected in the theater in other ways. Two of the sensational topics in the first half of 1861 found their way to the London stage. Within three weeks of Blondin's debut at the Crystal Palace, the Grecian Theatre put on a farce called simply *Blondin* (17 June), and in the following March the Strand Theatre mounted a dramatic sketch, *Caught in a Line; or, The Unrivalled Blondin*. Within months of the conclusion of the Yelverton case, the Lyceum Theatre produced (19 August) Edmund Falconer's comedy, *Woman; or, Love Against the World*, whose plot turned on the controversial issue of the Irish marriage law which prohibited a legal marriage between persons of different religious faiths.

The genial way the mid-Victorian theater had of making comic use of serious dramas was reflected in two responses to *The Colleen Bawn*. Melodrama was converted into burlesque in *The Colleen Drawn* (Surrey Theatre, 14 October 1861) and into farce in *The Colleen Bawn Settled at Last* (Lyceum, 5 July 1862). And the topical popularity of the very word "sensation" led to its adoption in such titles as those of the pantomime *Cinderella and the Sensation Slipper* (Queen's Theatre, Edinburgh, 26 December 1861), the farce *A Great Sensation* (Sadler's Wells, 3 May 1862), and the extravaganza *Sense and Sensation; or, The Seven Saints of Thule* (Olympic Theatre, 16 May 1864).

Joining Boucicault's more or less original melodramas on the London stage were plays based on best-selling sensation novels. At the very moment that the term "sensation drama" was entering the theatrical vocabulary, a dramatization of Wilkie Collins's sensation novel (not yet so called), *The Woman in White*, was performed at the Surrey Theatre (3 November 1860); by the time the term had gained wide currency, another version was staged at Sadler's Wells (19 August 1861). Two of Mary Elizabeth Braddon's most successful sensation novels,

Lady Audley's Secret (1862) and *Aurora Floyd* (1863), were adapted by several playwrights. There are records of at least four versions of the first, beginning with two within a single week (the Queen's Theatre, 21 February, and St. James's Theatre, 28 February 1863). Five different adaptations of *Aurora Floyd* were produced in London houses between 11 February and 21 April of the same year.

Yet, curiously enough, few melodramas seem to have been inspired by the twin sensational events of July 1861. In their time, equally celebrated crimes such as Thurtell's murder of Weare, William Corder's of Maria Marten (the Red Barn sensation of 1827), and James Blomfield Rush's of Isaac Jermy in 1849 had been profitably represented on stage, and even now revivals or fresh versions of those hastily cobbled melodramas were being produced for the benefit of a new generation of playgoers. But no plays are recorded whose titles suggest that they were deliberately meant to exploit the fame of the 1861 cases. There was no *Major Murray's Ordeal; or, The Spider Web in Northumberland Street* at the Lyceum or the Adelphi, and no *The Baron and His Son; or, The Deadly Assault in the Surrey Lane* at the Surrey (across the river) or the Britannia in the East End.

Still, even if no play had a plot fully based on the story of Major Murray's involvement with William Roberts through the innocent but almost fatally misguided agency of his pretty mistress, the English stage had reason to be grateful to the stout-hearted officer. The struggle in which he ultimately prevailed was one more instance of life imitating art. Fierce hand-to-hand combats between hero and villain had been a staple of melodrama for many years; now the newspapers documented, as it were, such events, giving them uncontestable credibility whenever they were staged thereafter. Not only credibility: extra excitement, stemming both from the novelty of the setting—a locked room in the midst of London—and from the lavishness of the weaponry employed. The Northumberland Street struggle became a prototype of stage fights in later Victorian blood and thunder drama. Whether the plot line leading to the climactic fight occasionally bore some resemblance to the historic one is impossible to determine without a laborious search for such few of the scripts as may survive. It appears, though, that as the Murray-Roberts fight passed into legend its circumstances were drastically revised, in the theater if not in public memory. Some stage versions presented both men as scoundrels, Murray being a solicitor who had engineered a shady deal for which Roberts blackmailed him. In any event, one evidence of the persistence of the now fabled combat in the theater was the production at the Standard Theatre, Shoreditch, on 10 April 1882 of a melodrama titled *Humanity; or, A Passage in the Life of Grace Darling*, a grotesque but not untypical grafting onto a single plot of two famous episodes separated by almost a quarter-century. One of the first instant celebrities created by the media, Grace was a light-house keeper's daughter who heroically (it was said) rescued several persons from a shipwreck that occurred near her father's post in 1838. During the few short years she lived after her deed she was an object of public adulation, and after her death in 1842 her memory was kept green by, among other means, sentimental ballads and melodramas. In the play of 1882, two of the voyagers she rescued were villains, clearly modeled after the received figures of Murray and Roberts. The last act was devoted to the evil warriors' fight, which ended in their killing each other, to the gratification of the falsely accused, who rushed in to find bodies as the police had found Roberts's body in his devastated chambers. Some years after this monstrosity was performed in Shoreditch, the last act was detached from it and acted separately as an eighteen-minute sketch, with one of the villains recast as a Jewish hero who sang a song called "Only a Jew." This innovation did not, however, mitigate the fury of the fight. A fresh supply of china, glass, and lightweight furniture had to be bought for each performance.

CHAPTER FIVE

The Novel Experience

The "sensation" in the melodrama of the 1860s involved not only the addition of athletic and mechanical devices as sources of excitement but the historical context in which these were presented. In deference to a shift in the audience's tastes, playwrights had been gradually turning away from stories laid in the past and making a point and virtue of locating their actions in the present time. This intensified interest in using the stage as a mirror of contemporary life affected the melodrama as much as it did other theatrical genres. Now that realistic sets were available to reproduce the visual aspects of modern everyday life, sensation dramatists were able to present melodramatic events, new or from stock, in plausible settings, the novelty of which was itself a sensation. In enlisting what might be called "the shock of actuality"—of recognizable present-day scenes and characters in contemporary dress—as opposed to "romance," which implied another time, another locale, the sensation drama sought to authenticate the unlikely plot and the extraordinary incidents of which it was composed. And this is what sensation fiction also sought to accomplish, on the printed page.

Again, it was the label that was new, not, for the most part, the product itself. The sensation novel was a not too precisely differentiated subgenre of fiction distinguished by a high content of melodramatic narrative. Readers in quest of agreeable shocks had been well served, in their respective times, by the Gothic tale of terror, Sir Walter Scott's romances with their copious perils, accidents, and confrontations, and popular fiction, mostly historical romances, by such of Scott's successors as William Harrison Ainsworth. Whatever other powerful appeals they had, Dickens's novels were devoured for their frequent use of melodramatic situations and events—the "circle of fire," as Ruskin called it—which brought the thrills of the theater to the fireside. In 1868, George Augustus Sala, writing in the *Belgravia* magazine (edited, incidentally, by the reigning monarch of sensation fiction, Miss Braddon), pointed out what should have been obvious seven years earlier, when the term was first applied to fiction:

> The only wonder is that the charitable souls [some of Dickens's critics] have failed to discover that among modern "sensational writers" Mr. Charles Dickens is perhaps the most thoroughly, and has been from the very outset of his career the most persistently, "sensational" writer of the age. There is sensation even in *Pickwick*: the "Madman" and the "Stroller's" story, the death of the "Chancery Prisoner," and the episode of the "Queer Client," for example. *The Old Curiosity Shop* is replete with sensation, from the extravagant pilgrimage of Nell and the old man to the death of Quilp. *Barnaby Rudge* begins with the sensation of an undiscovered murder, and ends with the sensation of a triple hanging and a duel *à mort*. In *Nicholas Nickleby* the end of Mr. Ralph Nickleby and the shooting of Lord Frederick Verisopht by Sir Mulberry Hawk are sensational enough to suit the strongest appetite. And the murder of Tigg Montague by Jonas Chuzzlewit; and the mysterious husband of Miss Betsy Trotwood in *David Copperfield*; and the convict millionaire in *Great Expectations*; and the grinding of the "National Razor" in the *Tale of Two Cities*; and Monks's confession, and the murder of Nancy, and the death of Sykes, in *Oliver Twist*; and finally, the spontaneous combustion in *Bleak House*;* and the tumbling down of the house in *Little Dorrit*; and Mr. Carker's death in *Dombey and Son*. Are not all these pure "sensation"?

Sala's catalog illustrates how broadly the term had come to be applied by that time. But most of its examples fall into two categories, secrets on which the plots hinge and violent deaths, especially murders. These had been familiar components not only of some fiction read by the middle classes, including the "Newgate novels" (narratives of criminal careers) by Bulwer-Lytton and Ainsworth, but the

---

*Dickens considered several titles for the novel before he decided on *Bleak House*. Among them was not *Lady Dedlock's Secret*, which would have contributed to the strong case that could be made for *Bleak House* as a proto-sensation novel.

flood of cheap pot-boiled fiction for the lower-middle and working classes, the crude pabulum that scandalized many concerned observers of the cultural scene.

Although many novels published before 1860 qualified as examples of sensation fiction, the first new one to be so called was Wilkie Collins's *The Woman in White*, which was serialized in Dickens's weekly paper, *All the Year Round*, between 26 November 1859 and 25 August 1860, published in book form in the latter month, and reissued in one volume in 1861, just months before the Murray and Vidil affairs (the preface was dated February). It is not certain as yet just when the adjective was first extended from the drama to fiction, but an allusion to the genre in the *Morning Herald*'s valedictory to the Vidil case on 25 August shows that it was current by that time: "the moral disorganisation of which all classes in society are now complaining, and which forms the staple of most of our sensation novels."

Less than a year later, in *Blackwood's Magazine* for May 1862, the term was so well established as to serve as the title of a double-columned twenty-page review, by the well-known novelist Margaret Oliphant, of *The Woman in White* and Dickens's *Great Expectations*, which latter book she explicitly called a "sensation novel" because of its "incidents all but impossible, and in themselves strange, dangerous, and exciting." Buyers of *All the Year Round* had been reading the last weekly installments of the novel the preceding summer. Magwitch, the returned convict, had revealed his secret to an appalled Pip in the issue for 25 May. On 22 June, just a week before Baron de Vidil attacked his son, Miss Havisham, still dressed in her decayed bridal gown, suffered fatal burns in a fire at Satis House. On 6 July there was an account of Pip's perilous confrontation with the murderous Orlick; and on 13 July—the very day that the newspapers carried the first reports of the two sensations—the issue of *All the Year Round* that was being snatched up at the newsagents' and bookstalls contained the climactic event of *Great Expectations*, Pip's and Herbert Pocket's attempt to smuggle Magwitch out of the country, which ended in the melodramatic night scene of the rich old convict being fatally injured during a death struggle with the evil Compeyson under the keel of a speeding Thames steamer. Even before the novel's serial run was concluded on 3 August, the finished book had been published and was reviewed on the weekend of 20 July in the *Examiner* and the *Saturday Review*, side by side with their editorials on the two great crimes of the moment.

Dickens's latest novel, therefore, the work of the era's most popular writer of fiction, provided an immediate literary background to the developing sensation craze. (It is possible that the writer of the *Standard*'s editorial on the Vidil case on 22 July, referring to the public's reluctance to undergo "the ordeal of wasting whole days in the company of policemen and about the purlieus of the police courts, attended by the knowing clerk of a gentleman most improperly designated the 'thieves' attorney,'" had Wemmick and Jaggers in mind.) *Great Expectations*, like *Bleak House* (1852–53), had been intended, as Dickens said in the preface to the latter, to dwell "upon the romantic side of familiar things," a phrase that might well stand as a definition of what the ensuing school of sensation novelists was about.

And school it was—an informal collection of novelists, men and women, mostly second-rate or worse, unified in their sense of what the reading public most wanted at the moment and their readiness to oblige. In April 1863, a long review-essay in the *Quarterly Review* by the philosopher and historian Henry Mansel, dealt with no fewer than twenty-four examples of sensation novels, including two or three, published in 1859–60, to which the name was applied retroactively. Although sensation fiction, so called, continued to be ground out as late as the 1880s, the vogue reached its peak in the mid-1860s. An unidentified writer in the *Westminster Review* (October 1866) described its hectic intensity and scope as well as anyone:

> There is no accounting for tastes, blubber for the Esquimaux, half-hatched eggs for the Chinese, and Sensational novels for the English. Everything must now be sensational. Professor Kingsley sensationalizes History [in *Hereward the Wake*], and Mr. Wilkie Collins daily life. One set of writers wear the sensational buskin, another the sensational sock. Just as in the Middle Ages people were afflicted with the Dancing Mania and Lycanthropy, sometimes barking like dogs, and sometimes mewing like cats, so now we have a Sensational Mania. Just, too, as those diseases always occurred in seasons of dearth and poverty, and attacked only the poor, so does the Sensational Mania burst out only in times of mental poverty, and afflict only the most poverty-stricken minds. From an epidemic, however, it has lately changed into an endemic. Its virus is spreading in all directions, from the penny journal to the shilling magazine, and from the shilling magazine to the thirty shillings volume.

Preeminent in the shoal of lesser writers who swam in the wake of Collins and Dickens in those first years of the sensation craze was

Mary Elizabeth Braddon, whose *Lady Audley's Secret*, serialized in the monthly *Sixpenny Magazine* from January to December 1862 and published in three volumes in October of the same year, was regarded by contemporary critics as the prototype of the new genre. Henry James, indeed, credited Miss Braddon rather than Collins with having "created the sensation novel." It was a huge success at the circulating libraries, eight editions being called for during the first three months after publication in book form. The novel was full of appropriately thrilling accessories, such as a secret passage in a country house (a holdover from innumerable Gothic romances) and a thunderstorm in which lightning plays around the razors of a gentleman's dressing case, "a phenomenon," said a reviewer, "of which we never heard before, and shall never read of again except in a 'sensation' novel."

But these were trivial matters. The two daring features that set *Lady Audley's Secret* apart from preceding melodramatic fiction and, through it, determined the nature of the sensation novel to come were the figure of the beautiful Lady Audley, a female Mephistopheles as one critic called her, and the crimes she either committed or contemplated. At a time when, in crime-ridden fiction, women were almost always cast in victimized roles—Marian Halcombe and Laura Fairlie in *The Woman in White*, for instance—she was depicted as an out-and-out villain. By that single stroke, Miss Braddon defied convention, challenging the prevailing estimate of women as angels in the house, almost by definition incapable of crime, and of murder least of all. Lady Audley was the prey of murderous instincts, and if she failed to achieve her goal of killing her first husband, it was not for want of trying: she threw him down a well, and it was not her fault that, unknown to her, he managed to climb out and escape to America. She did succeed in being an arsonist on one occasion. Both murder and arson, however, were commonplace crimes, even if not ordinarily associated with women. Lady Audley's third crime, by contrast, was bigamy, a violation of law one party to which was of necessity a woman. Two distinguished novels had set a precedent for the use of this comparatively rare crime as plot material. In *Jane Eyre* (1847) Mr. Rochester, his insane wife still living, made an abortive attempt to marry Jane. And in *Pendennis* (1848–49) Lady Clavering was married to her second husband in the erroneous belief that her first, a convict named Amory, was dead. Thackeray got her out of her difficulty by revealing that her first marriage was no marriage at all, Amory having already become a multiple bigamist with wives scattered from Newcastle to New Zealand. Moreover, in the past three years the murder trial of the bigamous Dr. Smethurst and the Yelverton case had sharpened public enthusiasm for stories whose complications mirrored the real-life ones that had been exposed at the Old Bailey and in the Dublin courtroom, and while *Lady Audley's Secret* was running in the *Sixpenny Magazine*, *All the Year Round* was serializing Collins's *No Name*, which also hinged on the issue of whether a marriage had legal force.

Bigamy quickly became a spécialité de la maison in sensation fiction; of the twenty-four novels Mansel listed in his *Quarterly Review* article, no fewer than eight had plots hinging on that titillating crime.

> No novel [said the *Westminster* reviewer, 1866] can now possibly succeed without it. In real life money is sometimes obtained by marriage, but in literature only by bigamy. When Richardson, the showman, went about with his menagerie he had a big black baboon, whose habits were so filthy, and whose behaviour was so disgusting, that respectable people constantly remonstrated with him for exhibiting such an animal. Richardson's answer invariably was, "Bless you, if it wasn't for that big black baboon I should be ruined; it attracts all the young girls in the country." Now bigamy has been Miss Braddon's big black baboon, with which she has attracted all the young girls in the country. And now Mr. Wilkie Collins has set up [in *Armadale*] a big black baboon on his own account.

Beyond bigamy lay a tract of liberal conduct that novelists and their reviewers could only hint at, in novels, said Mansel, "which, instead of multiplying the holy ceremony, betray an inclination to dispense with it altogether. . . . The chief interest centres on a heroine whose ideas on this subject are rather on the side of defect than of excess." Although the novelists who introduced such spicy hints of sexual irregularity doubtless valued them for their scandalous potential, they also discovered that they supplied useful plot material. As a reviewer in *The Reader* (3 January 1863) observed, "Unlawful passions are inevitably replete with a variety of sensational situations, of which authorized love, however fervent, is devoid, and the consequence is that a sensation novel which cannot dwell upon seductions, intrigues, infidelities, and illegitimate connections, is like Hamlet, not only without the Prince, but without the Ghost and without Ophelia."

The final ingredient in the sensation brew was relatively conventional. The sensation drama might have an element of mystery and detection—the legendary Hawkshaw appeared in Tom Taylor's *The Ticket of Leave Man* in 1863—but it could do well enough without it so long as suspense was supported by other means. In sensation fiction the element of secrecy, to be followed in due course by revelation, was considerably more important, often taking the form of guilty knowledge or missing documents. But the mysteries that engaged the patrons of the circulating libraries were mysteries of event, not of motive. Here the imaginative reach of journalism far exceeded that of popular fiction. We have seen the newspaper commentators playing amateur psychologist as they speculated on the motives behind the baron's and Roberts's murderous conduct, especially on the possibility of madness. In the Vidil trial, Serjeant Ballantine pursued as far as he could a line of inquiry tending to suggest that the son suffered from an unbalanced mind. But although the sensation novelists made madness a frequent visitant in their pages (Lady Audley attributed her criminal impulses to paroxysms of insanity, and she ended her days in a Belgian madhouse), they used it merely as a convenient plot device, not as a mysterious abnormality to be described and examined. In the sensation novel formula, suspenseful plot and exciting incident were all, character nothing. The men and women, usually titled, endowed with the social graces and adequate money, and dressed in the latest fashion, served only as puppets to advance the story and as models for the book's engraved illustrations. Few of them, Wilkie Collins's sometimes excepted, had the three-dimensional authenticity of the dauntless major, his devoted mistress, the fixated Roberts, the adventurous baron, or his neurotic son, or, for that matter, the reality of the miscellaneous witnesses who were tangled by accident in a pair of sensational proceedings in law. The depth and variety of psychological interest that lend so much permanent vitality to the fiction of Dickens, Thackeray, the Brontës, Trollope, and George Eliot were alien territory to the sensation novelists of the 1860s and after.

Nor were they concerned with probability; the strange but (as it proved) true story of Major Murray dispensed them from the obligation that normally binds the writer of realistic fiction. Thackeray was right: "After this, what is not possible?" The plain evidence of the newspapers was infinitely more impressive than Dickens's specious effort to justify the wild coincidences he so freely employed when they were needed. In Northumberland Street crumbled into dust the limits placed on the degree to which novelists—not romancers, but writers purporting to mirror contemporary life—were entitled to strain their readers' credulity. In sensation fiction the timely distribution of accidents, barring the supernatural, knew no bounds. If Dickens could invoke "scientific" authority for the spontaneous combustion that incinerated the junk dealer Krook in a shop not far from Fleet Street, or if Wilkie Collins and Trollope could avail themselves of obscure legal quirks for plotting purposes, sensation novelists had behind them the undeniable precedent of Northumberland Street.

What lent the final piquancy to all these bold deviations from the prevailing line of morality and the ordinary odds of likelihood was the implication, deliciously terrifying to every reader of sensation fiction, that they could happen to you and me, if not as actual participants then as vitally interested witnesses. Henry Mansel, writing ironically at the moment, made the same observation that had flowed from the pens of newspaper writers in the summer of 1861, dwelling on the peculiarly modern flavor of the Murray and Vidil cases: "The man who shook our hand with a hearty English grasp half an hour ago—the woman whose beauty and grace were the charm of last night, and whose gentle words sent us home better pleased with the world and with ourselves—how exciting to think that under these pleasing outsides may be concealed some demon in human shape, a Count Fosco [in *The Woman in White*] or a Lady Audley!"

Henry James put it more picturesquely two years later, when, in the pages of the American *Nation* (9 November 1865), he credited Wilkie Collins with "having introduced into fiction those most mysterious of mysteries, the mysteries which are at our own doors. This innovation gave a new impetus to the literature of horrors. It was fatal to the authority of Mrs. Radcliffe and her everlasting castle in the Apennines. What are the Apennines to us, or we to the Apennines? Instead of the terrors of *Udolpho*, we were treated to the terrors of the cheerful country-house and the busy London lodgings. And there is no doubt that these were infinitely the most terrible. Mrs. Radcliffe's mysteries were romances pure and simple; while those of Mr. Wilkie Collins were stern reality. . . . Of course, the nearer the criminal and the detective are brought home to the reader, the more lively his 'sensation.'"

James's jaunty tone was at odds with the deeper concerns expressed, or implicit, in what his English contemporaries wrote on the same subject. It was no light matter to see fell purposes and deeds attributed to the social class that by the mid-Victorian era had become the prime wielder of political, social, and economic power and the center of attention in imaginative literature, above all fiction: the self-consciously and proudly moral middle class. Its primary interest in literary matters was to read about itself, to find its comfortable world mirrored in fiction. To the distress of most arbiters of taste and morality in such matters, it did not resent the action of sensation novelists in revealing its world to be not so comfortable and safe after all. In fact, the welcome it gave to sensation fiction was striking evidence that it actually relished so drastic a shattering of its illusions. Ironically, in an era when most novelists worshiped, in behalf of their readers, at the altar of domesticity, sensation novelists turned the reverential ideal of home and family inside out, purporting to discover lurking behind the innocent façade of decorous life a prodigious quantity of illicit behavior.

During its feverish run in the 1860s, sensation fiction did not enjoy a very good press, though occasional critics minimized its defects even if they did not linger to praise it. Moral objections aside, the main charge against the genre was that it was written for, and devoured by, a middle-class clientele whose literary taste should be the exemplar of wholesomeness, proof against the seductions of romancers. In sensation fiction, the principal ingredients of the despised street literature, stories that sold in penny and halfpenny slices, moved up-market, so to speak, finding their way into staid households and corrupting the imaginations of susceptible readers. "These tales," said Mansel, "are to the full-grown sensation novel what the bud is to the flower, what the fountain is to the river, what the typical form is to the organised body. They are the original germ, the primitive monad, to which all the varieties of sensational literature may be referred." The customary reading fare of the workingman did have its counterpart in sensation fiction, but Mansel was indulging in a grossly oversimplified form of literary genetics: the sensation novel also had a far more reputable ancestry. But by the 1860s, cheap working-class fiction, which had previously depicted crime for its shock value alone, ironically was hedged with a certain morality, its authors purporting to depict it only to warn against its dangerous allure. In the sensation novel, by contrast, it went unreproved. Whatever purposes the authors had in mind did not include any ambition to strengthen their readers' moral principles.

It was this spectacle of the solid, educated middle class accepting and indeed reveling in the sensation novelists' picture of its own corruption that the archbishop of York deplored when he spoke before the Huddersfield Church Institute in the autumn of 1864. In an address widely reported in the newspapers (the *Times* for 2 November, for example, devoted a whole long column to it), he denounced the genre for the immoral influence it supposedly exerted on its readers. By implicitly glorifying crime as a frequent occurrence in the everyday life of the class to which they belonged, it tempted them to commit crimes themselves, or, if they were less suggestible, at least induced them to look upon other people's crimes with callous indifference rather than suitable revulsion. Sensation novels, the archbishop continued, "want to persuade people that in almost every one of the well-ordered houses of their neighbours there was a skeleton shut up in some cupboard; that their comfortable and easy-looking neighbour had in his breast a secret story which he was always going about trying to conceal; that there was something about a real will registered in Doctors' Commons and a false will that at some proper moment should tumble out of some broken bureau."

The *Times* reported that the audience responded to this observation with laughter, an indication of the spirit in which it was both offered and received. The archbishop, allowing himself to descend to drollery for a moment, was simply restating in an up-to-date context the ancient charge, heard in every Puritan campaign against a literary target since Tudor times, that fiction was to be eschewed because it provided a gravely false picture of actuality. There was no truth, he maintained—and by their laughter his auditors seemed to subscribe to its absurdity—in the impression that sensation novelists conveyed, of a respectable, mentally healthy middle class rife with melodramatic secrets, demonic creatures garbed in frock coats or crinolines, and criminal impulses.

But, as we have seen, the Murray and Vidil cases had induced newspaper commentators to adopt a quite different view: the everyday presence of dark mysteries and of social corruption was not a figment of sensation novelists' diseased imaginations but a hard fact to be faced. The newspaper coverage of the cases dramatically substantiated the premise that crime, including murderous assaults on the person, could very well occur in settled, highly respectable social circumstances. Like their colleagues in the somewhat more raffish profession of the theater, where sensation dramas were likewise sometimes set in fashionable society, the novelists found in the daily press constant warranty for the implied message, "it can happen to you," which added immeasurably to their stories' appeal.

Like the journalists who sought to read larger significance in particular criminal events, the people who commented at length on the popularity of sensational fiction freely generalized about what it seemed to imply about the national character at the moment, whether or not its picture was true to the facts. Both parties shared a common anxiety: what would the French, Britain's severest critics, think of that character as revealed, on the one hand, by the prevalence of crime and the workings of the English system of justice, and on the other, by sensation novels? Margaret Oliphant's voice (in *Blackwood's Magazine* for August 1863) was typical:

> Supposing our French neighbours were likely to judge us, as we are greatly apt to judge them, by the state of national affairs disclosed in our works of fiction, these lively observers must inevitably come to the conclusion that murder is a frequent occurrence in English society, and that the boasted regard for human life, which is one of the especial marks of high civilisation, exists only in theory among us. The charm of killing somebody, of bringing an innocent person under suspicion of the deed, and gradually, by elaborate processes of detectivism, hunting out the real criminal, seems to possess an attraction which scarcely any English novelist can resist.

"For the service of the modern novelist," Mrs. Oliphant said, "every species of moral obliquity has been called in to complicate the never-ending plot."

> What is piquant on the other side of the Channel is out of the question within "the four seas." We turn with a national instinct rather to the brutalities than to the subtleties of crime. Murder is our *cheval de bataille*; and when we have done with the Sixth Commandment, it is not the next in succession which specially attracts us. The horrors of our novels are crimes against life and property. The policeman is the Fate who stalks relentless, or flies with lightning steps after our favourite villain. The villain himself is a banker, and defrauds his customers; he is a lawyer, and cheats his clients—if he is not a ruffian who kills his man. Or even, when a bolder hand than usual essays to lift the veil from the dark world of female crime we give the sin itself a certain haze of decorum, and make that only bigamy which might bear a plainer title. . . . Murder, conspiracy, robbery, fraud, are the strong colours upon the national palette. . . . Law predominates over even romance and imagination. If we cannot frame a state of affairs unexceptionably right, which is impossible to humanity, we can at least take refuge in the construction of circumstances which are legally and punishably wrong; and this expedient seems satisfactory to the national conscience.

Was this truly, then, to borrow the phrase Trollope would later use as the title for a novel, the way we live now? On the whole, the observers analyzing the Murray and Vidil cases had more to say on the topic of the national malaise of which they were taken to be symptoms than did the critics of sensational fiction. The latter were concerned instead with the morality of the genre and its presumed effects on that of its readers. The sternest view was Mansel's, who called it one of the "morbid" phenomena of contemporary literature, "indications of a widespread corruption, of which they are in part both the effect and the cause; called into existence to supply the cravings of a diseased appetite, and contributing themselves to foster the disease, and to stimulate the want which they supply."

Of the several major authors who wrote fiction with a sensational cast, Collins was the only one to whom the term "sensation novelist" was customarily applied during his lifetime. He went on to exploit the fashion he had helped stir in *No Name* (1862), *The Moonstone* (1868), and several later, less successful novels. In *The Moonstone* occurs one of the few recognizable fictional uses of the Northumberland Street episode, a half-and-half mixture of fact and invention.* One Friday, Geoffrey Ablewhite meets a perfect stranger in a bank in Lombard Street; he is lured to an apartment at the back of the first floor of a house in (yes) Northumberland Street; while he has his back turned to the closed folding doors communicating with the front room he is assaulted. So far, except for shifting the scene of the initial encounter, Collins was faithful to the Murray story. But in other respects he freely adapted it. The room that in real life was cluttered with Louis Philippe furnishings became almost empty, apart from "a faint odour of musk and camphor" and "an ancient Oriental manuscript, richly illuminated with Indian figures and devices, that lay open to inspection on the table"; instead of being shot, Ablewhite is blindfolded, gagged, and searched, but not otherwise harmed by his attacker, one of three mysterious Orientals who had rented the apartment a short time earlier; and he is summoned to Northumberland Street by letter, not to receive an offer of a large loan to the Grosvenor Hotel Company but with the prospect of a large donation to the Mothers'-Small-

---

*There had already been a faint echo of Northumberland Street in Trollope's *Can You Forgive Her?* (1864–65). The rivals for Alice Vavasor's hand, her villainous cousin George and the loyal, steady John Grey, fight in the latter's rooms over a tailor shop in Suffolk Street, Pall Mall. In a return engagement, George actually tries to shoot Grey with a pistol.

Clothes-Conversion Society, a charity devoted to redeeming fathers' trousers from the pawnbroker and preventing their further use as collateral by altering them to fit a child. It is Ablewhite, not his assailant, who is found when "two respectable strangers" break into the room where he is bound to a chair. But the authentic flavor of the first phase of the Murray case comes through when he asks them, "What does it mean?" and they reply, "Exactly the question we were going to ask you." For good measure, Collins has the polite stranger whom Ablewhite met in the bank, Septimus Luker, fall into the hands of the three Orientals on the same day and under identical circumstances, this time in a byway off the Tottenham Court Road. Like Charles Reade, another sensation novelist who has some place in the history of Victorian fiction but not on the same level as Collins and (above him) Dickens, Collins heeded the sardonic advice critics repeatedly offered to the aspiring sensation novelist: "Let him only keep an eye on the criminal reports of the daily newspapers, marking the cases which are honoured with the special notice of a leading article, and become a nine-days' wonder in the mouths of quidnuncs and gossips; and he has the outline of his story not only ready-made, but approved beforehand as of the true sensation cast."

In *Our Mutual Friend* (1864–65), the novel that followed *Great Expectations*, Dickens used a variety of sensational material, and in fact may have drawn the outlines of the plot involving Bradley Headstone, the "respectable" schoolmaster whose mind has "gloomy and dark recesses" and outside his hours of work "broke loose . . . like an ill-tamed animal," from the story of William Roberts. The parallels are striking. Headstone is as obsessed with young Lizzie Hexam as Roberts was with Mrs. Murray, and in trying to locate her he shadows her lover and protector, Eugene Wrayburn, as relentlessly as Roberts shadowed Mrs. Murray. At the climax of the action, at the Plashwater Weir Mill lock on the Thames, Headstone waylays Wrayburn and attacks him with a murderous ferocity reminiscent of the Northumberland Street confrontation, but his badly injured victim, like the major, manages to survive.

Dickens was well into writing what might have been the most sensational of all his novels, appropriately titled *The Mystery of Edwin Drood*, when he died in 1870. Meanwhile, Trollope had fallen into the mode, though in his autobiography he would be at pains to distinguish his "realistic" fiction from the "sensation fiction" of writers whom he regarded as his antagonists. The plot of *Orley Farm*, published in monthly numbers in 1861–62, hinged on a disputed will, and many of Trollope's succeeding novels would contain incidents, if not actual story lines, that were obviously crafted in deference to the public demand. Thomas Hardy was affected by the sensation vogue at the outset of his career, and echoes of it are found in isolated episodes in most of his novels, half a dozen of which, for example, use murder as a plot device. Even the fastidious George Eliot was not exempt from the fever; there are elements of sensationalism in both *Felix Holt* (1866) and *Daniel Deronda* (1876–77). The most enduring heritage of the sensation fiction of the 1860s is found in these scattered aspects of Trollope's, Hardy's, and Eliot's novels. Recent critics have discovered there significant indications of the way the realistic impulse developed in English fiction and affected its form from 1860 onward.

The sensation vogue constituted a colorful and curious chapter in the history of English popular literary culture. Perhaps it would not have had the same impetus, or taken the shape it did, had its earliest pages not been in process of composition at that moment in July 1861 when the newspapers blazoned the occurrence of two real-life sensations in a single day's editions. In unconscious collaboration, Roberts, the driven loan shark, and Baron de Vidil, the somewhat dubious intimate of French royalty and English peers, set the tone, if not the stage, for the Victorian Age of Sensation.

BIBLIOGRAPHICAL NOTE

Very little has been written on either the Murray or the Vidil affairs. The best description of the former is in one of the chapters of Sir John Hall's *The Bravo Mystery and Other Cases* (New York, 1925). An earlier, amateurish treatment is in Canon J. A. R. Brookes's *Murder in Fact and Fiction* (New York, n.d.); the chapter entitled "Baffled Murderers" also glances at the Vidil case. (I am indebted to Jonathan Goodman for directing me to these sources.) The few scrappy pages in H. Chance Newton's *Crime and the Drama, or Dark Deeds Dramatized* (London, 1927; reprinted Port Washington, N.Y., 1970) are totally unreliable. The chapter on Baron de Vidil in Horace Wyndham's *Crimes in High Life: Some Society Causes Célèbres* (New York, 1927; British title, *Judicial Dramas*) has several details not found elsewhere.

The catalog of the British Library lists an imperfect copy of a pamphlet issued at the time of the Vidil sensation with the title *Baron de Vidil . . . His Life . . . Giving Particulars in Connection with the Charge of Attempting to Murder His Son*. But this item is reported to have been destroyed by bombing in the Second World War, and no other copy has been located.

A lively and authoritative description of the sensation craze, as well as of the sensation novel viewed as a popular literary subgenre, is Kathleen Tillotson's essay "The Lighter Reading of the Eighteen-Sixties," which forms the introduction to the Riverside edition of Wilkie Collins's *The Woman in White* (Boston, 1969). In its more analytical approach, Winifred Hughes's *The Maniac in the Cellar: Sensation*

Novels of the 1860s (Princeton, 1980) supplements the Tillotson essay and at the same time largely supersedes the pioneer study by Walter C. Phillips, *Dickens, Reade, and Collins, Sensation Novelists* (New York, 1919).

INDEX